TRAVERSE
THEATRE

TRAVERSE THEATRE COMPANY IN PARTNERSHIP WITH
EDEN COURT AND THE MACROBERT

PASSING PLACES
A Road Movie for the Stage

Youth / Alex's Mum / Iona / Mo	Mabel Aitken
Mirren	Iona Carbarns
Kid / Lollipop Man / Gunn / Petrol Pump Attendant / Walker / The Shaper	Callum Cuthbertson
Alex	Paul Thomas Hickey
Youth / Diesel / Serge / Tom / Barman	John Kazek
Binks	Peter Kelly
Brian	Colin McCredie

with music composed and performed by Mick Slaven

Director	John Tiffany
Designer	Neil Warmington
Lighting Designer	Chris Davey
Movement Director	Marisa Zanotti
Voice Coach	Ros Steen
Re-lights	Garry Ferguson
Stage Manager	Nils den Hertog
Deputy Stage Manager	Kay Courteney-Chrystal
Assistant Stage Manager	Victoria Paulo
Wardrobe Supervisor	Lynn Ferguson
Wardrobe Assistant	Alice Taylor

First performed at the Traverse Theatre Tuesday 4 February 1997;
first performance of this production Friday 10 April 1998
*The tour of PASSING PLACES is made possible by Barclays Stage Partners,
a sponsorship scheme from Barclays and the Scottish Arts Council.*

PLAYWRIGHT'S NOTE

Ten years ago my friend Robert and I were nursing hangovers and orange juices in Fauldhouse Miners Welfare when we decided to drive to Thurso. Simple as that. We drove through the night up the A9 and reached John O'Groats at dawn. We had breakfast in Thurso then spent two days meandering back down the west coast via Ullapool. The most memorable thing about the whole trip was the amazing sense of 'otherness' everywhere north of the Great Glen.

Over the next five years I made the trip to Caithness and Sutherland a number of times, on my own and with a variety of companions. Thurso revealed itself as a place of world importance for both surfers and nuclear physicists - home to the best waves in Europe and Dounreay power station. This bizarre overlap of different worlds was fascinating, likewise, the central belt's love affair with American culture and the West Highlands' reputation as a bolt-hole for disaffected city-dwellers.

I started constructing a story around these elements and fell into the notion of a Scottish road movie even though I had no access to film. The Traverse suggested I consider telling it on the stage - specifically, on the large, flexible and well-equipped stage in the theatre's new subterranean home. With a bit of imagination - and a decent budget - this idea came to seem increasingly possible. I realised my story of dislocation had found a home.

Several false starts, drafts and workshops later, PASSING PLACES finally took to the road. It's never looked back. So, whether you're a first-time traveller or a seasoned veteran, the advice is the same. Buckle-up, break out the barley-sugars and make sure you've been to the toilet. I hope you enjoy the journey.

Stephen Greenhorn
March 1998

Stephen would like to thank...

Debbie Cox, Rae Gilchrist, David Grieg, David Harrower, Guy Hollands, Zak Rankine, the teams at 7:84, the Traverse and both sets of actors who workshopped the script.

TRAVERSE THEATRE

Over the last thirty five years Edinburgh's Traverse Theatre has had a seminal influence on British and international theatre. With quality, award-winning productions and programming, the Traverse receives accolades at home and abroad from audiences and critics alike.

Traverse productions have been seen world-wide. Most recently, WIDOWS toured the UK and BONDAGERS toured the world, delighting audiences in London, Toronto and Budapest. After sell-out Edinburgh runs MOSCOW STATIONS transferred to both the West End and New York; UNIDENTIFIED HUMAN REMAINS and POOR SUPER MAN transferred to London's Hampstead Theatre; and after touring the Highlands and Islands of Scotland KNIVES IN HENS transferred to a sell-out season at the Bush Theatre in London.

1997 saw great success for the Traverse with the world premieres of Stephen Greenhorn's PASSING PLACES (on tour during Spring 1998), the Highlands and Islands tour of Iain Crichton Smith's LAZYBED, and the highly acclaimed GRETA - James Duthie's first work for the stage. No stranger to awards, the Traverse won ten awards at the 1997 Edinburgh Festival Fringe, including a Fringe First and Scotland on Sunday Critics' Award for Mike Cullen's ANNA WEISS.

As Scotland's new writing theatre, the Traverse is a powerhouse of quality experimentation, artistic diversity and the place to see the most important contemporary theatre. The Theatre commissions the best new writers from Scotland and around the world, facilitates numerous script development workshops, rehearsed readings and public writing workshops, and aims to produce five major new theatre productions plus a Scottish touring production each year.

An essential element of the Traverse Company's activities takes place within the educational sector, concentrating on the process of new writing in schools. The Traverse is unique in its exclusive dedication to new writing, providing the infrastructure, professional support and expertise to ensure the development of a sustainable and relevant theatre culture for Scotland and the UK.

BIOGRAPHIES

MABEL AITKEN (Youth / Alex's Mum / Iona / Mo): Trained RSAMD. For the Traverse: SHINING SOULS, THE LIFE OF STUFF. Other theatre work includes: GODODDIN (Test Department); THE CRUCIBLE, UNCLE VANYA, MIRANDOLINA (Royal Lyceum); THE EVIL DOERS (Winged Horse); HUGHIE ON THE WIRES (Calypso); THE WISHING TREE (Wiseguise); CUTTIN' A RUG (Young Vic); TWO SEVENS CLASH, COME ON (Damage); ALL IN THE TIMING (Nottingham Playhouse); THE LIFE OF STUFF (Donmar Warehouse); CONFEDERACY OF FOOLS (Germany). Radio work includes: THE CONFIDENCE, THE BELL IN THE TREE, BILL AND COO. Television work includes: RAB C. NESBITT, NERVOUS ENERGY, BETWEEN THE LINES, HAMISH MACBETH, WHERE THE HEART IS (BBC); SEARCHING. Film work includes: FEVER PITCH, WANTING AND GETTING, NERVOUS ENERGY, THE LIFE OF STUFF, STAND AND DELIVER.

IONA CARBARNS (Mirren): Trained: RSAMD. For the Traverse: LAZYBED, ANNA WEISS. Theatre work includes: THE MAIDEN STONE, SLEEPING BEAUTY (Royal Lyceum); TARTUFFE, HAVING A BALL (Perth Rep); QUIET NIGHT IN (KtC); Theatre Workshop's touring Christmas show. Radio work includes: PASSING PLACES (BBC). Film includes: WHEELS (Barony Films).

CALLUM CUTHBERTSON (Kid / Lollipop Man / Gunn / Petrol Pump Attendant/Walker / The Shaper): For the Traverse; LAZYBED. Recent theatre work includes: SPEED THE PLOUGH (Arches / Mayfest); QUIET NIGHT IN (KtC). Television work includes: RAB C NESBITT, STRATHBLAIR, ENGLISH EXPRESS, RUFFIAN HEARTS (BBC Scotland); HIGH ROAD (STV); WISE MEN (Channel 4). Film work includes: BREAKING THE WAVES (Zentropa); HOW HIGH THE CASTLE WALLS - also writer (Fallingwater Films).

CHRIS DAVEY (Lighting Designer): For the Traverse: GRETA. Theatre work includes: SHINING SOULS (Peter Hall Company at the Old Vic); THE CHERRY ORCHARD (Method & Madness); JANE EYRE, THE MILL ON THE FLOSS, THE DANUBE, DESIRE UNDER THE ELMS (Shared Experience); BROTHERS OF THE BRUSH, HAPPY VALLEY (Everyman, Liverpool); THE ILLUSION (Royal Exchange, Manchester); CAUSE CELEBRE, THEN AGAIN (Lyric, Hammersmith); MYSTERIA, EVERYMAN, THE COMEDY OF ERRORS, EASTER (Royal Shakespeare Company); THE TEMPEST, WAR AND PEACE (Royal National Theatre / Shared Experience). Opera work includes: THE PICTURE OF DORIAN GRAY (Opera de Monte Carlo); SCHUMANN SONG CYCLES (Batignano Opera, Tuscany).

GARRY FERGUSON (Re-lights): For the last two years Garry has been the Assistant Production Manager for the Royal Lyceum Theatre Company, Edinburgh. Prior to this he was Chief Technician for Tramway in Glasgow where he worked with, among others, Michael Clark, Robert Lepage, The Wooster Group, Peter Brook, The Mali Theatre of St Petersburg and DV8. Between leaving Tramway and joining the Lyceum Garry toured extensively in the UK and Europe with Communicado, The Wrestling School and Romanian companies, the National Theatres of Cluj, Craiova and Bucharest.

PAUL THOMAS HICKEY *(Alex)*: Trained: RSAMD. For the Traverse: PASSING PLACES, THE ARCHITECT. Other theatre work includes: SAILMAKER, TWELFTH NIGHT (TAG); ONE FLEW OVER THE CUCKOO'S NEST, MACBETH, STILL LIFE, ECSTASY, WASTED (Raindog); MERLIN THE MAGNIFICENT, THE ADVENTURES OF ARTHUR (Cumbernauld); JUMP THE LIFE TO COME (7:84 Scotland); THE SLAB BOYS TRILOGY (Young Vic); SHINING SOULS (Peter Hall Company at the Old Vic); TIMELESS (Suspect Culture). TV work includes: CARDIAC ARREST (BBC); TAGGART, HIGH ROAD, THE BRITOIL FRAUD, THE JACOBITES (STV); THE SWEETEST FEELING (Starcatch). Radio work includes several plays for BBC Radio Scotland including: BATTLE OF THE AIRWAVES, BODIES OCCUPATION, THE BASEMENT TAPES, SCOTTISH RESOURCES, ROCK & ROLL PEARLS, PASSING PLACES. Film work includes: CAFE RENDEZVOUS, WANTING AND GETTING, THE LUCKY SUIT, CALIFORNIA SUNSHINE, LAY OF THE LAND

JOHN KAZEK *(Youth / Diesel / Serge / Tom / Barman)*: For the Traverse: THE CHIC NERDS, STONES AND ASHES, EUROPE. Other theatre work includes: MACBETH, A DOLL'S HOUSE (Theatre Babel); MARABOU STORK NIGHTMARES (Citizens', Leicester Haymarket); MARY QUEEN OF SCOTS GOT HER HEAD CHOPPED OFF, KIDNAPPED, CARLUCCO AND THE QUEEN OF HEARTS (Lyceum); DIAL M FOR MURDER (Dundee Rep); LOOT, DRIVING MISS DAISY, CAN'T PAY, WON'T PAY (Byre); ORPHANS (Harbinger); NAE PROBLEM, GOVAN STORIES, JUMP THE LIFE TO COME (7:84); AS YOU LIKE IT, KING LEAR (Oxford Stage Co.); GREAT EXPECTATIONS (Lyric, Belfast); JUST FRANK (Theatre Royal, Stratford East). Television and film work includes: RAB C NESBITT, PUNCH DRUNK, DOUBLE NOUGAT, NERVOUS ENERGY, STRATHBLAIR (BBC); ALBERT AND THE LION (STV); SILENT SCREAM (Antonine Productions); RIFF RAFF (Parallax Pictures).

PETER KELLY *(Binks)*: For the Traverse: THE HARDMAN, WALTER, ANIMAL. London theatre work includes: BROTHERS KARAMAZOV, THE GOVERNMENT INSPECTOR, CRIME AND PUNISHMENT, CORIOLANUS, MASTER CLASS, THE POSSESSED. Other theatre work includes: TWELFTH NIGHT, THE CAUCASIAN CHALK CIRCLE (Royal Lyceum); THE TEMPEST (Shared Experience); season at the Citizens'. Television work includes: A TOUCH OF FROST, MINDER, TAGGART, DR FINLAY, LOVEJOY, THE BILL, EASTENDERS, THE LOVE BOAT. Film work includes: THE TALL GUY, WELCOME TO SARAJEVO, SURVIVING PICASSO, BEING HUMAN. Radio work includes: MACBETH, A SOLDIERS TALE, THE HOUSE. Work in Italy includes: Zefferelli's YOUNG TOSCANNINI, BLU NOTTE, LA PIOVRA, COINS IN THE FOUNTAIN.

COLIN McCREDIE *(Brian)*: Trained: RSAMD. For the Traverse: PASSING PLACES. Other theatre work includes: LUST (Etcetera, London); TEECHERS (Byre); GLENGARRY GLEN ROSS (Arches). Television work includes: TAGGART, DR FINLAY (STV); THE MISSING POSTMAN (BBC Scotland). Film work includes: SHALLOW GRAVE (Figment Films); SMALL FACES (BBC Films); THE PEN (Navigator Films); DOOM AND GLOOM (N.F.T.S.); CHARMED (E.V.T.C.); KARMIC MOTHERS (Fresh Films).

MICK SLAVEN (Musician): Plays guitar for Glasgow band THE LEOPARDS and records for CREEPING BENT RECORDS. The L.P. THEY TRIED STAYING CALM was released in October '97. Singles include: BURNING, THEME E, CUTTING A SHORT DOG and the forthcoming release STARLINES.

ROS STEEN (Voice Coach): Trained: RSAMD. For the Traverse: THE CHIC NERDS, GRETA, LAZYBED, KNIVES IN HENS, PASSING PLACES, BONDAGERS, ROAD TO NIRVANA, SHARP SHORTS, MARISOL, GRACE IN AMERICA, BROTHERS OF THUNDER. Other theatre work includes: THE DYING GAUL, CONVERSATION WITH A CUPBOARD MAN, EVA PERON, LONG DAY'S JOURNEY INTO NIGHT, SHADOW OF A GUNMAN, A TASTE OF HONEY, THE TINKER'S WEDDING, RIDERS TO THE SEA (Citizens'); ODYSSEUS THUMP (West Yorkshire Playhouse); BABYCAKES (Clyde Unity); ABIGAIL'S PARTY (Perth Rep); PYGMALION, OUR COUNTRY'S GOOD, ARMSTRONG'S LAST STAND (Royal Lyceum); TRAINSPOTTING (G & J Productions); THE HANGING TREE, LAUNDRY, ENTERTAINING ANGELS (LookOut); SUNSET SONG (TAG); BOLD GIRLS (Theatre Galore). Film work includes: STELLA DOES TRICKS. Television work includes: HAMISH MACBETH, LOOKING AFTER JOJO, ST ANTHONY'S DAY OFF, CHANGING STEP.

JOHN TIFFANY (Director): Trained: Glasgow University. Literary Director at the Traverse since June 1997. He directed GRETA, PASSING PLACES, SHARP SHORTS and co-directed STONES AND ASHES for the Traverse. Other theatre includes: HIDE AND SEEK and BABY, EAT UP (LookOut); THE SUNSET SHIP (Young Vic); GRIMM TALES (Leicester Haymarket); EARTHQUAKE WEATHER (Starving Artists). Film includes: KARMIC MOTHERS (BBC Tartan Short) and GOLDEN WEDDING (BBC).

NEIL WARMINGTON (Designer): Graduated in Fine Art at Maidstone College of Art before attending the post-graduate theatre design course at Motley. For the Traverse: PASSING PLACES (TMA Nominated Best Design). Recent theatre credits include: THE DUCHESS OF MALFI (Bath); JANE EYRE (Shared Experience); WOMEN LAUGHING (Watford); THE TEMPEST (Contact, Manchester); DESIRE UNDER THE ELMS (Shared Experience); ANGELS IN AMERICA (7:84 Scotland); TROILUS AND CRESSIDA (Opera North); HENRY V (Royal Shakespeare Company); MUCH ADO ABOUT NOTHING (Queen's Theatre, Shaftesbury Ave); THE LIFE OF STUFF (Donmar Warehouse); LIFE IS A DREAM (TMA Award Best Design), FIDDLER ON THE ROOF (West Yorkshire Playhouse); WAITING FOR GODOT, MUCH ADO ABOUT NOTHING (Liverpool Everyman); THE GLASS MENAGERIE, COMEDIANS, MERLIN (Parts 1 & 2) (Royal Lyceum); BLITHE SPIRIT (York Theatre Royal); I PUT A SPELL ON YOU (Leicester Haymarket); CORIOLANUS (Tramway); CRAZYHORSE (Paines Plough); OEDIPUS REX (Harvard State Opera). He has also won The Linbury Prize for stage design and The Sir Alfred Munnings Florence prize for painting.

MARISA ZANOTTI (Movement Director): Trained: The Laban Centre, London in dance theatre. She is Artistic Director of Anatomy Performance Company, a Glasgow-based company specialising in multi-disciplinary work. Commissioned pieces include: 16/17 (Tramway); RUNNER (CCA); 15 MINS - 6 HOURS (New Moves); ANATOMY. Her work has been seen at festivals in Britain, Spain, Quebec and America. As a performer she has worked with The Cholmondeleys, Laurie Booth and Wendy Houstoun. Movement direction for theatre includes: PASSING PLACES (Traverse); SLEEPING AROUND (Paines Plough); ELEKTRA (Diva / Tramway). Film work includes four broadcast dance films with The Cholmondeleys and a commission with director Katrina MacPherson to make PACE forBBC2's *Dance For The Camera* season.

The Traverse would like to thank the original cast of PASSING PLACES:

Stuart Bowman, Kenneth Bryans, Paul Thomas Hickey, Kathryn Howden, Veronica Leer, Iain Macrae, Colin McCredie and, lighting designer, Ben Ormerod.

PASSING PLACES props, costumes & scenery built by Traverse workshops
Funded by the National Lottery

for PASSING PLACES:
Scenic Artist: Rachel George
Production Photography: Kevin Low
Print Photography: Euan Myles
Passing Places Map Illustration: Duncan Nicoll

Wardrobe Care: LEVER BROTHERS

For generous help with PASSING PLACES the Traverse Theatre thanks:

Charlie Ingle, City of Edinburgh Council • City of Edinburgh Property Services Department • Edinburgh Military Tattoo Ltd • Mach Enterprises • Bob Dickson • Bank of Scotland • BHS, Princes Street • PhoneIn, George Street • Shakespeare's Return Public House • The Hermitage Public House • Morag MacLleod and the School of Scottish Studies • K.J.P. Photographics • Kodak UK Ltd • Unique Events • G.I. Joes, Dalry Road • Lee at Gilbarco Ltd., Halifax • Oddbins, Bruntsfield • McDonalds Restaurants Ltd. • The Original Kitchen Design Company • Cardinal Sports Ltd. • Traverse Bar Cafe • Royal Lyceum Theatre • Dundee Rep Theatre

TRAVERSE THEATRE • THE COMPANY

Annie Bambach
Kitchen Assistant

Maria-Theresa Bechaalani
Deputy Electrician

Stephen Bremner
Assistant Bar Manager

Christian Cappelle
2nd Chef

Calum Chaplin
Head Chef

Kay Courteney-Chrystal
Deputy Stage Manager

Vian Curtis
Production Technician

Emma Dall
Finance Assistant

Rachel Davidson
Deputy Bar Manager

Nils den Hertog
Stage Manager

Janet Dick
Cleaner

Anjo Duffy
Kitchen Assistant

Lynn Ferguson
Wardrobe Supervisor

Michael Fraser
Theatre Manager

Anne Gerhaghty
Assistant Administrator

Mike Griffiths
Production Manager

Paul Hackett
Finance Manager

Noelle Henderson
Development Manager

Philip Howard
Artistic Director

Ruth Kent
Assistant Box Office Manager

Mark Leese
Design Associate

Niall Macdonald
Bar Manager

Jude MacLaverty
Marketing/Box Office Assistant

Justin McLean
Administrative Assistant

Jan McTaggart
Marketing & Press Officer

Lucy Mason
Administrative Producer

Lorraine May
Front of House Manager

Alex Musgrave
Box Office Manager

Victoria Paulo
Assistant Stage Manager

Renny Robertson
Chief Electrician

Hannah Rye
Literary Assistant

Kirstie Skinner
Assistant Administrator

Richard Stembridge
Production Assistant

Fiona Sturgeon
Marketing Manager

John Tiffany
Literary Director

Ella Wildridge
Literary Associate

ALSO WORKING FOR THE TRAVERSE
Felix Balfour, Anna Copp, Andrew Coyle, Ben Ewart-Dean, Sarah Jane Dooley,
Connie Fullerton, Linda Gunn, David Henderson, David Inverarity, Ian Jack,
Katherine Johnston, Judith Keston, Linda Keys, Calum Macdonald, Jamie
MacPhee, Nadine Mery, Rory Middleton, Duncan Nicoll, Graziano Pozzi, Michel
Quiniou, Joanna Stewart, Kate Tame, Jenny Temple, Nicole Wise, Robbie Wood,
Lynsey Wright

TRAVERSE THEATRE - BOARD OF DIRECTORS
Tom Mitchell President, **Sir Eddie Kulukundis** Vice President,
John Scott Moncrieff Chair, **Stuart Hepburn** Vice Chair,
Scott Howard Secretary, **Barry Ayre, Geraldine Gammell, Muriel Murray**

SPONSORSHIP

Sponsorship income enables the Traverse to commission and produce new plays and offer audiences a diverse and exciting programme of events throughout the year.

We would like to thank the following companies for their support throughout the year.

⚜ **BANK OF SCOTLAND** ESPC

CORPORATE ASSOCIATE SCHEME

LEVEL ONE

Balfour Beatty
Basilica Computing Ltd
Scottish Life the PENSION company
United Distillers

LEVEL TWO

Laurence Smith - Wine Merchants
NB Information
Métier Recruitment
Willis Corroon Scotland Ltd

LEVEL THREE

Allingham & Co, Solicitors
Alistir Tait FGA Antique & Fine Jewellery
Gerrard & Medd, Designers
KPMG
Nicholas Groves Raines Architects
Scottish Post Office Board

With thanks to

Navy Blue Design, designers for the Traverse and to George Stewarts the printers. Robin Arnott of the Royal Bank of Scotland for his advice on information technology and systems.
This placement was arranged through Business In The Arts.
Purchase of the Traverse Box Office and computer network has been made possible with funds from the National Lottery.

The Traverse Theatre's work would not be possible without the support of

THE SCOTTISH ARTS COUNCIL.   ·EDINBVRGH·
                                 THE CITY OF EDINBURGH COUNCIL

The Traverse receives financial assistance for its educational and development work from

Calouste Gulbenkian Foundation, Esmee Fairbairn Charitable Trust, The Peggy Ramsay Foundation, The Nancie Massey Charitable Trust, John Lewis Foundation, Scottish International Education Trust, Save and Prosper Educational Trust

Charity No. SC002368

for Mandy...

...who was driven round the bend
and still paid for the taxi home.

PASSING PLACES

A Road Movie for the Stage
by
Stephen Greenhorn

Characters
ALEX
BRIAN
MIRREN

BINKS, *Motherwell gangster*
KID, *Motherwell delinquent*
IONA, *Canadian geologist*
SERGE, *French sculptor*
DIESEL, *English traveller*
TOM, *Mirren's dad*
SHAPER, *mystic surf guru*
MO, *Cornish surfer*

FIRST YOUTH
SECOND YOUTH
QUIZ MASTER
ALEX'S MUM
LOLLIPOP LADY
SMALL BOY
GUNN
PUMP HAND
LADY WALKER
BARMAN

1

ALEX *and* BRIAN *enter.*

ALEX. Motherwell!

BRIAN. West central Scotland. Population 27,000.

ALEX. Work base . . .

BRIAN. Traditionally . . . heavy industry . . . predominantly steel . . .

ALEX. And now . . .

BRIAN *shrugs.*

ALEX. Alright . . . Famous for . . .

BRIAN. Winning the Scottish Cup in extra time?

ALEX. And . . . ?

BRIAN. And!

ALEX. Surfing.

BRIAN. Oh. Yeah. Surfing.

ALEX. Motherwell. Surf City. The Bondi Beach of Lanarkshire.
Malibu of the North.

BRIAN. Ideally situated.

ALEX. Twenty-five miles from the fucking sea!

2

The shop. Doorbell goes as the KID *enters. Thirteen going
on thirty.*

ALEX. What do you want?

KID. Chill man. I've been saving up. I'm looking for a new pair
of Air Jordans?

ALEX. How much have you got?

KID. Here.

KID *slaps a bunch of notes on the counter.*

ALEX *counts them.*

ALEX. Not enough. Unless you're one-legged.

KID. Aw no. What about instalments?

ALEX. Aye. You can buy one shoe now and hop it.

KID. Very funny.

ALEX. Away and mug somebody.

KID. Nobody round here worth mugging.

ALEX. Beat it then.

KID. Cool the beans, pal. I'm going. But I'll be back.

He goes to the door.

KID. Here.

ALEX. What?

He waves sarcastically.

KID. There's a wee wave for your surf-board.

ALEX. Get to fuck!

KID *exits laughing.* ALEX *regards the surf-board.*

ALEX. Two years that bastard thing's been in the window. Two years! And I've had to dust it every second day. All because he thinks he's the Don-fucking-Jonson of Meikle Earnock!

BRIAN *interjects from the Library.*

BRIAN. Three hundred and twelve!

ALEX. Eh?

BRIAN. Three times a week for two years not counting holidays.

ALEX *scowls at him.*

ALEX. The library! Hang out for pensioners who can't pay their gas bills. Ex-steelworkers who can't bring themselves to watch Australian soap-operas. Jakeys who fall asleep over The Independent . . . And Brian!

BRIAN. I was just saying!

3

Shop doorbell interrupts. BINKS *enters.*

ALEX. Mr. Binks, I thought . . .

BINKS. Shut it, arse-face.

He goes behind the counter, rakes for an empty shoe box then takes a hand-gun from his waistband, wraps it and stashes it in the box. He stores the box back under the counter. ALEX *is staring.*

BINKS. What're you looking at?

ALEX. Nothing.

BINKS. That's right. And don't you . . . Eh? . . . Aye.

ALEX. Sorry?

BINKS. Am I speaking to you!

ALEX. But you . . .

BINKS. Ronnie's saying you have to be deaf, dumb and blind to work here.

ALEX. Dumb anyway.

BINKS. Eh?

ALEX. Nothing.

BINKS. Dinnae mutter son. I cannae stand muttering.

ALEX. Sorry, Mr. Binks.

BINKS *moves to the surf-board. He strokes it.*

BINKS. When was the last time you dusted my wee beauty here?

ALEX. Yesterday.

BINKS. Do it again.

ALEX. But . . .

BINKS. Again, I said!

ALEX. It . . . eh . . . it doesn't have a price on it.

BINKS. That's cause it's not for sale, ya retard. Right?

ALEX. So if anyone asks about it . . . ?

BINKS. Are you deaf? It's not for fucking sale. This is my retirement. My pension plan. In a few years time me and Ronnie and this wee beauty'll be jetting off to a beach house in Hawaii. So long Lanarkshire, hello Honolulu! Wearing flowery shirts, chasing birds in grass skirts, drinking Buckie out of half-coconuts. Fucking paradise.

ALEX. Aye.

BINKS. So make sure you run a fucking duster over it before I come back this afternoon.

Eh? . . . Aye. Right enough, Ronnie . . . Dumb! Dumb as a . . . doorbell.

He exits.

ALEX. Fucking psycho.

BRIAN. Mr Binks is subject to a bizarre paranormal phenomenon whereby he is in constant contact with the spirit of his twin brother who died at birth.

ALEX. Shite.

BRIAN. Not necessarily.

ALEX. He's barking. Nothing but a mental sports shop owner. And it's not even a real sports shop. All it sells are trainers and baseball caps. And bloody shell-suits. The only people who ever come in are all –

4

Shop doorbell again. Two YOUTHS *enter.*

ALEX. Like Sauchiehall Street in here! Can I help you?

SECOND YOUTH. We're looking for baseball caps.

ALEX. By the window.

FIRST YOUTH. Right.

SECOND YOUTH. Your shop?

ALEX. I just work here.

SECOND YOUTH. Been busy?

ALEX. Not bad.

They pick out a couple of hats.

FIRST YOUTH. We'll take these.

ALEX. Anything else?

FIRST YOUTH. Bats.

ALEX. Bats?

SECOND YOUTH. We're thinking of starting a team.

ALEX. Yeah?

ALEX *places a baseball bat on the counter. One of the youths picks it up.*

FIRST YOUTH. This is good. Nice weight.

SECOND YOUTH. That'll do then.

ALEX. Anything else?

SECOND YOUTH. Yeah.

ALEX. What?

SECOND YOUTH. Everything.

    ALEX *is whacked with the bat and thumps to the floor.*

BRIAN. And that's where all the trouble started . . .

5

BINKS *enters the ransacked shop. He checks first that the board is okay then that his gun is still there. It is. Only then does he try to revive* ALEX.

BINKS. Wake up ya wee prick.

    ALEX *groans.*

BINKS. I don't think he's listening, Ronnie . . . Aye. Good idea.

He hauls a concussed ALEX *to his feet and gives him a shake.*

ALEX. Mr. Binks.

BINKS. Something you want to tell me, son?

ALEX. God. What a mess.

BINKS. That's right. A real mess. In my shop. So maybe you could explain it, before I get angry and Ron gets violent . . . He says he wants your knee-caps for castanets. And I don't like to deny him his little treats.

ALEX. Two guys. Young guys. I've never seen them before. They came in for baseball caps then they wanted to look at a bat . . .

BINKS. And you gave them one?

ALEX. They said they were starting a team.

BINKS. Ron says he can guess what happened next.

ALEX. They clubbed me over the head.

BINKS. Ahh. And does it hurt?

ALEX. Aye. It does.

BINKS. Good! I hope they've fractured your fucking skull! I hope you've got fucking brain damage! Except, I don't think you've got a brain to damage!

ALEX. I tried to stop them but they . . .

BINKS. They had the fucking bat that you gave them ya clown! And while you were in Noddy-land they made a home run with the till and most of my stock.

ALEX. Sorry.

BINKS. You will be.

ALEX. Have you phoned the police?

BINKS. So they can come round and have a good laugh too?

ALEX. Well, what are you going to do then?

BINKS. I'm going to boot your arse out that door . . . Or mibbe the window, Ronnie's suggesting.

ALEX. Are you saying I'm fired?

BINKS. Wasn't I clear enough for you?

ALEX. But what about my money. I'm due wages.

BINKS. They were in the till, weren't they. Looks like you got robbed too.

ALEX. That's not fair.

BINKS. Tough.

6

ALEX *and* BRIAN *are in a pub.* ALEX *is very drunk,* BRIAN *only slightly less so. There is a trivia quiz going on in which* BRIAN *is trying to participate.*

ALEX. See, what gets me . . . what gets me, right, is he really thinks he's a gangster or something.

BRIAN. He is.

ALEX. Well, I know. But he thinks he's Al Pacino. Scarface or something. Michael Corleone.

QUIZ. C'mon now folks get the scores sorted. One round to go.

BRIAN. They've taken a point off cause we spelt Azerbaijan wrong. Nine out of ten.

ALEX. Bastard thinks he's in a big movie.

BRIAN. Still third. I think we can win if we have a good last round.

ALEX. Don't you think you've had enough?

QUIZ. Last round, ladies and gentlemen. And it's ten questions on . . . Sport.

BRIAN. Shit. Rangers players and greyhounds!

ALEX gets up to go.

ALEX. I've had enough of this. You coming?

BRIAN. Okay. Okay.

They stumble away from the table.

QUIZ. Which former Rangers star now trains greyhounds?

7

In the street. Night. The two lads are weaving their way home through the empty pedestrian precinct.

ALEX. Look at this place. Nothing but shoe shops and burger bars.

BRIAN. I'm starving.

ALEX. IT DOES MY HEAD IN!

BRIAN. You'll have the cops doing your head in if you don't shut up.

ALEX. Huh. They're the same. Too many episodes of Miami Vice. Rush around going 'freeze'. And, 'make my day'! Half of them couldn't even make their beds.

BRIAN. Time to go home, I think.

ALEX. No. Wait. Look. The scene of the crime.

The sports shop. They peer through the wndow.

BRIAN. They really cleaned it out, didn't they.

ALEX. Took everything.

BRIAN. Except the surf-board.

ALEX. Left that just to piss me off.

BRIAN. Binks' pride and joy.

ALEX. Stupid psychedelic phallic symbol.

BRIAN. Must be worth a wee bit too.

ALEX. Three hundred and twelve. Not counting holidays. Skivvying for that prick. Makes me sick. Wouldn't even give me the money he owes me.

BRIAN. Forget it, Alex. There's nothing you can do.

ALEX. Is there not?

    ALEX *goes looking for something.*

BRIAN. Alex?

    ALEX *has found a litter bin.*

BRIAN. What're you doing?

    ALEX *grunts with effort as he lifts the bin up.*

BRIAN. Alex? Bloody hell!

An enormous crash as the litter-bin flies through the shop window. An alarm bell begins to clatter loudly. ALEX *scrunches through the broken glass.*

BRIAN. Fucking hell! What're you doing? Let's get out of here. Come on.

ALEX. Hold on.

BRIAN. Oh no. Alex. You can't take that.

    ALEX *is wrestling with the surf-board.*

ALEX. Can I not?

BRIAN. I don't believe this.

ALEX. Grab an end then!

    They pick the thing up.

ALEX. Surf's up!

They haphazardly make their escape into the night with the board. ALEX *laughing hysterically. The alarm ringing in their ears.*

8

Next morning. ALEX*'s house. The phone rings.* ALEX'S MUM *enters and answers it.*

MUM. Hello . . . Who's calling please? . . . Alright, I'll just get him for you . . .

    She switches off her 'telephone' voice.

MUM. ALEX!

ALEX. What?

MUM. Phone.

ALEX. Right.

Pause. ALEX *realises he is in bed with the surf-board.*

ALEX. Ohmygod!

He is panic stricken.

MUM. Alex!

ALEX. I'm not in.

MUM. It's Mr. Binks.

ALEX. Aaah! I'm not here. Tell him I've gone. Away. The Army. Or dead. Tell him I'm dead.

MUM. Alex . . . ?

ALEX. Just tell him I'm NOT HERE. Please!

MUM. Huh.

She goes back to the phone as ALEX *begins dressing and packing in a frenzy.*

MUM. I'm afraid he's not here Mr. Binks. He must've gone out already . . . Well to his work, I suppose . . . Oh. No, I didn't know that . . . Yes . . . I'll be sure to tell him . . . bye then.

She goes into the bedroom.

MUM. What the hell've you been up to?

ALEX. What did he say?

MUM. He said you got fired yesterday.

ALEX. And?

MUM. And! What d'you mean, 'and'?

ALEX. Did he say anything else?

MUM. Something about castanets.

ALEX. Oh God!

She spies the board.

MUM. Have you been nicking stuff from your work?

ALEX. No.

MUM. What's that then, a leaving present?

ALEX. Look . . .

MUM. Look nothing. I'm not having the polis at my door because of you. If you've got yourself into trouble you can get yourself out of here. I've warned you, you can pack your bags and . . .

She notices that ALEX *has done just that.*

MUM. Where are you going?

ALEX. Eh?

MUM. Oh aye. Spain, is it? Costa del Crime n'that, eh?

ALEX. Spain!

MUM. Castanets.

ALEX. No. Look. I just need to go away for a while. Trust me.

MUM. About as far as I could throw you.

ALEX. It's fine.

MUM. I'm not going through all that business again. D'you hear me?

ALEX. I hear you. I have to go.

    ALEX *clatters out with the board.*

MUM. Just like his father. Bastard.

9

BRIAN's *house.* BRIAN *is trying to dress.* ALEX *is trying to explain his plan.*

BRIAN. But couldn't we just take it back and offer to pay for the window?

ALEX. Are you off your fucking head!

BRIAN. Shut-up. You'll wake my dad.

ALEX. An earthquake couldn't wake your dad before the first race.

BRIAN. So what're we going to do?

ALEX. Get out of the way for a bit. Get rid of the evidence.

BRIAN. Where?

ALEX. North.

BRIAN. D'you think you could be a wee bit more specific?

ALEX. There's a place, I read about it in one of those magazines in the shop. It's full of all those surfing bastards. We could sell this and then use the money to lie low for a while.

BRIAN. What place is this then?

ALEX. Thurso.

BRIAN. Thurso! Do you know where that is?

ALEX. North. On the coast, I presume.

BRIAN. North is right. Next stop Iceland. How are we going to get up there with a surfboard?

ALEX. Aye well. I was thinking about that . . .

10

A car shrouded beneath a dust-sheet. ALEX *approaches it confidently.* BRIAN *is deeply wary.* ALEX *whips the sheet off to reveal a clapped out Lada Riva.*

BRIAN. Our George'll kill me.

ALEX. He'll understand.

BRIAN. He's not the understanding type.

ALEX. It's only a fucking Lada.

    ALEX *gets in.*

BRIAN. He can do things with his hands, you know. They train them. Cut off oxygen to the brain. Dead in under a minute.

ALEX. Brian. George is in the catering corps. The deadliest thing he can do with his hands is not wash them.

    ALEX *tries the engine. It starts reluctantly.*

ALEX. We're in business.

11

In the car. ALEX *drives, crunching gears occasionally.* BRIAN *is a nervous passenger.*

BRIAN. Are you insured for this?

ALEX. Maybe George's policy covers it.

BRIAN. What if we get stopped?

ALEX. It doesn't matter. It's not taxed either.

BRIAN. Oh god.

12

They stutter to a halt at a traffic light. ALEX *revs impatiently.*

ALEX. Come on. Change!

    The KID *enters and approaches them.*

KID. Hey! You that guy that works in the sports shop up the centre?

ALEX. No.

KID. Aye y'ur. You chucked me out of there yesterday.

ALEX. Should you not be at school?

KID. Should you not be at work?

ALEX. I retired. Piss off.

KID. Nice car! D'you know there's stuff dripping underneath at the front? What's on the roof? Skateboard for when you break down?

ALEX. I'm warning you. Beat it.

KID. Where're you going then? Scrappy?

BRIAN. Thurso.

ALEX. No!

KID. Make your minds up.

ALEX. Away and play on the motorway.

KID. I've more chance of getting there than you. Especially with ma new trainers.

ALEX. Where did you get them?

KID. Twenty quid. No questions.

ALEX. They're nicked!

KID. Should've let me join the Christmas club, eh?

    KID *runs off laughing again.*

ALEX. Prick.

    Car horn sounds impatiently behind them.

BRIAN. It's green. We can go.

    ALEX *crunches the gears again and they drive off.*

13

The remains of the shop. BINKS *sweeping up broken glass.*

BINKS. I'll kill the wee bastard when I get my hands on him. I will. I'll fucking kill him . . . Of course it was him. Who else would it be?

The KID *enters cautiously.*

KID. Hey mister. You missing a surf-board?

BINKS. What's it to you?

KID. I might know where it is.

The broom drops to the floor and BINKS *suddenly has the* KID *by the throat.*

KID. Aow!

BINKS. Talk or choke, Ron says. Up to you.

KID. I saw that guy who was working here with it. Him and his mate. They were in a car. A Lada. In town. The surf-board was tied to the roof.

BINKS. Bastards. I knew it!

KID. They were leaving. Said they were . . . going to . . .

BINKS. Where? Going where?

KID. My throat! I can't . . .

BINKS *relaxes his grip a little.*

BINKS. Where?

KID. Thurso.

BINKS. Are you sure?

KID. Aye.

BINKS. Bastards!

KID. Do I get a reward?

BINKS *ignores this. He is distracted by the information. His grip tightens on the* KID'*s throat. The* KID *starts to choke.*

BINKS. Thurso . . . Aye, Ronnie. Track them down . . . We'll get it back alright . . . Thurso, that's what he said . . . Well, I don't fucking know . . . I'll buy a map or something, alright? . . . What? . . . Eh? . . . Oh. Aye.

He lets go of the KID *who is barely conscious.*

BINKS. Thanks wee man.

KID. S'alright.

14

ALEX *and* BRIAN *in the car.*

BRIAN. It is!

ALEX. I'm not arguing.

BRIAN. Yes you are.

ALEX. I just thought Loch Ness was bigger.

BRIAN. But we're talking area. This is Loch Lomond. The largest area of fresh water.

ALEX. If you say so.

BRIAN. It is.

ALEX. Fine.

Pause.

ALEX. How far is it exactly?

BRIAN. Depends on which way you go.

ALEX. How many can there be?

BRIAN. Two. The obvious and the sneaky.

ALEX. And is the sneaky way very complicated?

BRIAN. Not if I'm navigating.

ALEX. You've got the map.

BRIAN. Okay. Another few miles up the A82, then take a left through to Arrochar on the A83, then . . .

ALEX. That's enough to be going on with.

BRIAN. It's a much more interesting route as well.

ALEX. We're not on holiday, Brian.

BRIAN. Closest I've been to a holiday for years.

ALEX. What about that weekend on Arran?

BRIAN. That was an Outward Bound course.

ALEX. So?

BRIAN. Not a holiday.

15

A lay-by in a mountain pass. The car bonnet is open. Steam rises.
ALEX *fumes.*

BRIAN. They're designed for Murmansk not Milngavie. It's
    meant to be traversing the icy wastes of Siberia. It's out of its
    natural environment. Give it a chance.

ALEX. Brian, how are we going to get to Thurso if this thing
    won't do more than forty-five and can't even get us over a
    fucking hill?

BRIAN. It's not a hill. It's a mountain. Three thousand three
    hundred and eighteen feet. That makes it a munro.

ALEX. I don't give a fuck.

    A beat.

BRIAN. It's only the radiator. We just have to wait for it to cool
    down, then top it up with fresh water.

ALEX. From where?

BRIAN. There'll be some around somewhere.

ALEX. How do you know?

BRIAN. It's the Highlands. There's always water.

    Pause.

ALEX. Where are we?

BRIAN. It's called 'Rest and be thankful'.

ALEX. Of course.

BRIAN. The top of the pass. It's the route of the old military road.
    Look, you can see /

ALEX. Where are we going?

BRIAN. Well . . .

ALEX. Doesn't that map tell you?

BRIAN. You've not quite got it yet, have you?

ALEX. Got what?

BRIAN. The whole concept.

ALEX. What concept?

BRIAN. Maps. Imaginary landscapes. Representations of the
    world. All the information's there. Everything you need to
    know. But you still have to prescribe your own course of
    action.

ALEX. What the fuck are you on about?

BRIAN. A map's not for telling you where to go. What it tells you is exactly where you are. It only describes your position. You have to decide your own destination and journey. See?

Pause.

ALEX. This is going to be a very long drive, isn't it?

16

Motherwell. BINKS *prepares to begin his pursuit. He is wearing motorcycle leathers.*

BINKS. Right, Ronnie. North. Time for payback.

He kickstarts a motorcycle and revs it.

What?. . . . Eh? . . . Aye alright. I'll no go too fast.

He lets out the clutch and screeches away.

17

In the car. BRIAN *in guide book mode.*

BRIAN. Inverary. A picturesque township on the shores of Loch Fyne. Notable for its carefully planned layout, its church tower and its historic court-house, now an award-winning museum.

ALEX. White-washed tourist hell-hole.

BRIAN. Excellent sea-fishing opportunities. In season.

ALEX. We're not stopping.

BRIAN. Hard right on to the B819 up and through Glen Aray.

ALEX. More hills.

BRIAN. Then down to the shore of Loch Awe.

ALEX. More water.

BRIAN. Loch Awe is the longest inland loch in Britain if you include the bit that goes off at right-angles. If you don't then Loch Ness is longest.

ALEX. More useless shite.

BRIAN. Left on to the A85 and towards Oban along the Pass of Brander. Past Ben Cruachan. They blasted a huge cavern under it and built a hydro-electric power-station completely underground.

ALEX. Fascinating.

BRIAN. You can go on guided tours.

ALEX. We're not stopping.

BRIAN. It has Britain's longest staircase.

ALEX. For fucks sake! It's like being on the road with Norris McWhirter!

BRIAN. I was just saying . . .

ALEX. We're not tourists, Brian.

BRIAN. I've not been here before.

ALEX. We live here.

BRIAN. Not here.

ALEX. We're only a hundred miles from Glasgow.

BRIAN. Yeah? Look though. See anything familiar?

ALEX. Only you talking shite.

18

A lay-by near Loch Creran. The car is again steaming. ALEX *sighs.*

ALEX. It's your turn to get the water.

BRIAN. I'll go in a minute.

ALEX. This is going to take fucking days.

BRIAN. There's no hurry, is there?

ALEX. Not at this rate there's not.

BRIAN. No point in getting harassed, then.

ALEX. You been reading those Yoga books again?

A pause. A noise outside. ALEX *sits up.*

ALEX. Someone's coming.

BRIAN. Eh?

ALEX. Look. Worzel McGummidge.

BRIAN. What does he want?

ALEX. How should I know?

> DIESEL *enters. A new-age traveller carrying a poached rabbit.* ALEX *and* BRIAN *get out of the car.*

DIESEL. Having problems?

ALEX. Just letting it cool down.

DIESEL. Radiator leaking?

ALEX. Aye. A wee bit. We have to top it up now and then.

DIESEL. Where are you headed?

BRIAN. Thurso.

ALEX. Maybe. We don't know.

BRIAN. We're just . . .

ALEX. Driving.

BRIAN. And stopping.

ALEX. I see.

> *A beat.*

DIESEL. And is that a surf-board?

ALEX. Sort of.

DIESEL. A sort of surf-board?

ALEX. Aye.

DIESEL. Why is it wrapped in bin-liners?

ALEX. Didn't want to get it wet.

DIESEL. Isn't it waterproof?

BRIAN. Acid rain. Damages the . . . the eh . . . thing.

DIESEL. Right.

> DIESEL *has a look under the bonnet.*

DIESEL. Have you been using the headlights on this?

ALEX. Eh aye. Of course. Why?

DIESEL. 'Cause you haven't got any.

ALEX. What!

DIESEL. There's no connections, or bulb mountings, or bulbs.

ALEX. Shit.

DIESEL. I think your battery's leaking as well. It probably won't be holding a charge. Could be your alternator's buggered too.

ALEX. Jesus.

BRIAN. Are you a mechanic?

DIESEL. Not really. I know a bit about engines though.

He comes out from under the bonnet.

ALEX. The name's Diesel.

BRIAN. I'm Brian. He's Alex.

DIESEL. How you doing?

BRIAN. Not very well, by the sound of it.

ALEX. Will it go?

DIESEL. To Thurso?

ALEX. To anywhere?

DIESEL. Not tonight.

ALEX. Shit.

Pause.

DIESEL. Have you got anywhere to stay?

BRIAN. The back seat.

DIESEL. Could you sleep in a tent?

BRIAN. Yeah.

DIESEL. Well, our camp's just down there. We could probably find you a blanket or two.

ALEX. You camping?

DIESEL. We're travellers.

ALEX. New age?

DIESEL. All different ages.

BRIAN. Are you sure it's not any trouble . . .

DIESEL. Nah. I can have a look at the car tomorrow if you like.

BRIAN. That'd be great. Eh?

ALEX. Yeah. Great. Thanks.

19

The travellers' camp. BRIAN *and* ALEX *describe.*

ALEX. The camp. A bus, two lorries, a caravan, a proper tent and a couple of home-made ones . . .

BRIAN. Benders.

ALEX. . . . Lots of facial hair. Two kids . . .

BRIAN. . . . and a baby . . .

ALEX. . . . a dog, two cats and a goat . . .

BRIAN. . . . called Maggie.

ALEX. Woodsmoke. Smells of cooking.

BRIAN. Rabbit stew. It was nice. With bread. They bake their own.

ALEX. Water from the stream and . . .

BRIAN. And her.

   ALEX *and* BRIAN *are by a campfire.* MIRREN *approaches and dumps some blankets beside them.*

MIRREN. These should keep you warm enough. The nights are fairly mild anyway.

BRIAN. Thanks.

   She sits down beside them.

BRIAN. I'm Brian, by the way. This is Alex.

MIRREN. Mirren.

BRIAN. That's a nice name. Is it Gaelic?

MIRREN. No. My dad chose it. He's from Paisley. Big football fan.

   Pause.

MIRREN. You're from Glasgow then?

ALEX. Motherwell.

MIRREN. On holiday?

ALEX. Not exactly.

MIRREN. Going to Thurso? For the surfing?

ALEX. No.

MIRREN. You've got a board.

ALEX. We're delivering it.

MIRREN. I didn't realise Motherwell had a big surfing scene.

BRIAN. It doesn't anymore. We've nicked it.

ALEX gives BRIAN a kick.

MIRREN. You on the run then?

ALEX. We're just taking the board to Thurso.

MIRREN. If you say so.

ALEX. I do.

MIRREN. I don't know what you're worried about. We're hardly likely to turn you in, are we? It's not as if you're the Great Train Robbers, is it?

She laughs. ALEX sighs.

ALEX. So he goes and tells her the whole story.

BRIAN. They were nice to us.

ALEX. She thinks it's a great laugh.

BRIAN. Well . . .

ALEX. Thinks we're a right pair of prats.

BRIAN. She doesn't.

ALEX. So much for keeping a low profile.

BRIAN. It wasn't a fucking press conference.

MIRREN laughing. DIESEL joins them by the fire.

DIESEL. What are you lot laughing about?

MIRREN. Nothing. How's the car?

DIESEL. Well, I've fished out an old battery and left it to charge off the van. It's not up to much but it's better than what you've got. It'll be ready in the morning. It should fit.

ALEX. Thanks.

DIESEL. You really need to replace some parts. I haven't got any for a Lada.

BRIAN. Are you sure you're not a mechanic?

DIESEL. Not really.

MIRREN. Your Lada's too lightweight for him. He used to fix tanks.

BRIAN. Tanks? Were you in the army?

DIESEL. For a bit.

MIRREN. Nine years.

DIESEL. Quite a bit.

BRIAN. So how did you end up here?

DIESEL. Couldn't settle. Ended up on the road. Met some other folk in the same boat. Moved around a bit. Headed north. Been here five months now. It's nice.

BRIAN. Are you planning to stay?

DIESEL. Till they move us on. They'll get round to it sooner or later. They always do.

Pause.

BRIAN. How long have you been on the road, Mirren?

MIRREN. Well . . . uhm . . .

DIESEL. Mirren's just visiting.

BRIAN. Oh.

DIESEL. Heading off soon as well. Maybe these guys could give you a lift.

MIRREN. You just said the car won't make it.

DIESEL. I might be wrong.

BRIAN. Where are you going?

DIESEL. Up to Tom's, isn't it? Tongue.

MIRREN. I don't think this . . .

DIESEL. That's on the way to Thurso.

BRIAN. It's right next door.

MIRREN. I was going to Skye first. To see Iona.

DIESEL. Even better idea! Serge might be just the man for Ladas.

BRIAN. I thought Iona was by Mull.

DIESEL. This one's a person. Lives on Skye with a weird French bloke – Serge. Always doing things with old cars. Lots of Ladas and Skodas and stuff. He's got loads of bits. He might be able to help you.

BRIAN. That sounds like a good idea.

ALEX. Skye?

MIRREN. It's a bit of a detour.

DIESEL. Rubbish. You go over at Mallaig and back on the bridge. No problem.

MIRREN. You've got it all worked out haven't you?

DIESEL. Makes sense. Two birds with one stone.

BRIAN. Go on, Mirren.

MIRREN. I don't want to hold you back.

BRIAN. You'd be doing us a favour, eh Alex?

ALEX. We don't want to put you to any trouble . . .

BRIAN. Please.

Pause. MIRREN *looks at* DIESEL.

MIRREN. Alright.

BRIAN. Brilliant. A guide. You can't beat local knowledge.

DIESEL. Sorted then.

MIRREN. Yeah. Sorted. Thanks, Diesel.

A beat.

MIRREN. I suppose if I'm going I'd better get my shit together.

She stands.

DIESEL. And I have to sort out some tent space for you two.

He stands too.

MIRREN. See you in the morning.

BRIAN. Night.

MIRREN *and* DIESEL *move away.*

MIRREN. I didn't realise you wanted rid of me.

DIESEL. You know it's not like that.

MIRREN. I thought . . .

DIESEL. I know. It's been good. But you can't stay.

MIRREN. Why not?

DIESEL. Because you're still looking for answers, Mirren. And there's none here for you.

They exit. ALEX *watches them go.*

ALEX. I don't think she wants to come with us.

BRIAN. Rubbish. It'll be great.

ALEX. You think?

20

Next morning. At the car.

MIRREN. Who's driving then?

ALEX. Me.

MIRREN. Will I go in the back?

BRIAN. I'll go. You go in the front.

MIRREN. Are you sure?

BRIAN. You can give directions better from there.

MIRREN. But if you've got a map . . .

BRIAN. No, honestly . . .

MIRREN. I don't want to be in the way.

BRIAN. You won't be.

MIRREN. But if you'd prefer . . .

BRIAN. Really, I don't mind . . .

ALEX. Will you just get in the fucking thing and we'll see if it starts.

They get in.

21

In the car. On the road. Later.

MIRREN. So, what's it like being outlaws then?

BRIAN. It's really interesting. We've never been this far North before.

MIRREN. Maybe you should have turned to crime sooner.

BRIAN. Yeah.

ALEX. It's not a joke. We're only here because we want to keep our knee-caps.

MIRREN. And where would you rather be?

ALEX. Right now, I'd settle for Thurso.

BRIAN. Skye first. What's the best way d'you think?

MIRREN. If you cross Loch Linnhe at the Corran ferry, you can go up to Mallaig without having to go through Fort William.

BRIAN. Sounds good.

ALEX. How far to this ferry then?

BRIAN. On the left just after the bridge at Ballachulish.

ALEX. Ballachulish.

BRIAN. Used to be a centre for quarrying slate. For roofs.

MIRREN. That's right.

BRIAN. They've got a new visitor centre too.

ALEX. We're not stopping.

22

BINKS *is in Fort William. He is by the road trying to attract the attention of a* LOLLIPOP LADY.

BINKS. Excuse me. Oi! Lollipop! Are you deaf?

LADY. Patience dear. We'll get you across in a minute.

BINKS. I don't want to cross the road.

LADY. What are you standing there for then?

BINKS. Are you on duty all day?

LADY. Not all day. Not quite. I have to get home before five for the cat.

BINKS. Have you seen two men in a Lada with a surf-board on the roof?

LADY. Pardon?

BINKS. Have you seen two men in a Lada with a surf-board on the roof?

Pause.

LADY. Ah. I know who you'll be.

BINKS. Eh?

LADY. You'll be from the Sunday Post, won't you? Asking trick questions and seeing if anybody recognises you.

BINKS. No.

LADY. You're supposed to give me some money if I know the right answer. Wait a minute now. It'll come to me. I was reading it just the other day . . .

BINKS. Look, I think you're . . .

LADY. Aw, come on now give me a chance. It's on the tip of my tongue.

BINKS. Will you listen . . . ?

LADY. Now, is it a fiver or a tenner you give me?

BINKS. I'm not the man from the Sunday Post!

LADY. Give us a wee clue, will you? I get it every week but my memory's not what it was. Go on. Tell me what to say.

BINKS. I don't want you to say anything.

LADY. I just get the money for recognising you?

BINKS. I'm not giving you any money.

LADY. Och. That's not fair. If you'd just give me time to think. Or a wee clue . . .

BINKS. Forget it. Just forget it.

LADY. But I get it every week. It's the cat's favourite too.

BINKS *is walking away, twitching.*

LADY. Ach. Ya tight bastard, ye.

BINKS. Mad as a fucking hatter . . . eh, Ronnie?

23

Corran ferry on Loch Linnhe.

ALEX. The Corran Ferry. Nearly a fiver to get across about a hundred yards of water.

BRIAN. What were you expecting? Deckchairs? Duty-free?

ALEX. What's wrong with a bridge?

MIRREN, ALEX *and* BRIAN *are looking over the side.*

MIRREN. Do you know where we are?

BRIAN. Middle of Loch Linnhe.

MIRREN. There's a mountain a few miles down the lochside there, at Glensanda.

BRIAN. Yeah?

MIRREN. They've shovelled most of it away to Europe. High quality aggregate to build the autobahns. To link Brussels and Bonn.

BRIAN. A whole mountain?

ALEX. There's plenty of them left. You surely wouldn't miss the one.

MIRREN. Sorry?

ALEX. Joke.

MIRREN. Oh.

Pause.

ALEX. So, what do you do exactly? For a living?

MIRREN. Lots of things.

ALEX. Nothing in particular.

MIRREN. Bits and pieces. Seasonal stuff in hotels and bars. Sometimes more interesting things.

ALEX. And you just drift from one place to another?

MIRREN. I move on when I get bored.

ALEX. Strange way of life.

MIRREN. Really? Stranger than kidnapping a surf-board?

A mini stand-off between the two. BRIAN *is relieved to be able to interrupt it.*

BRIAN. Land ahoy! Looks like the cruise is over!

24

On the road. Glen Tarbert. Single track with passing places.

BRIAN. A861 west through Glen Tarbert then along Loch Sunart. Through Strontian. Famous for lead mining. Gave its name to the element strontium which was discovered here in 1764.

MIRREN. They rehearsed the D-day landings on the loch here as well.

ALEX. Stereo now.

MIRREN. If you carried straight on you'd go into Ardnamurchan.

BRIAN. The most westerly point on the British mainland.

MIRREN. Very beautiful.

ALEX. We're going north.

BRIAN. Ardshealach. The end of Loch Shiel.

MIRREN. Blain.

BRIAN. Mingarrypark.

MIRREN. Dalnabreck.

BRIAN. Ardmolich.

MIRREN. Kinlochmoidart.

BRIAN. Kylesbeg.

ALEX. We're overheating again.

MIRREN. You or the car?

25

BINKS *is phoning home.*

BINKS. No . . . No ma . . . Fort William . . . Aye, Glen Coe was
   lovely . . . no, I'm not taking any pictures . . . I'm not on holiday, ma, it's a business trip . . . What? . . . Aye, alright I'll try
   and remember . . . but . . . look . . . I haven't got time to look
   for one wi a Highland Cow on it! . . . Sorry . . . No, I didn't
   mean to shout . . . aye, alright . . . Look, I have tae go . . . tae
   Inverness . . . Aye ye go along the loch . . . What? . . . But they're
   just stories ma . . . There's no really anything . . . Alright, okay,
   I'll keep an eye out . . . Right. I have tae go. Cheerio.

He hangs up.

BINKS. What is she like . . .

26

Outside the car waiting for it to cool.

BRIAN. What a view.

MIRREN. That's Muck. And Eigg. Rum behind that. And that's
   the Cuillins on Skye.

BRIAN. Doesn't look very far.

MIRREN. No not really.

BRIAN. You think your friend will be able to fix this?

MIRREN. Serge? I don't know.

BRIAN. What about Iona? What does she do?

MIRREN. She's a geologist. She's writing a book.

BRIAN. About what?

ALEX. Rocks.

MIRREN. Something to do with continental drift.

BRIAN. That's interesting.

ALEX. It's rocks.

Pause.

ALEX. It's a shame they couldn't use some of that high quality aggregate to improve the roads round here.

MIRREN. What's wrong with them?

ALEX. They're too narrow.

MIRREN. Single-track with passing places.

ALEX. They're crap.

MIRREN. They're fine. If you use them properly.

ALEX. Meaning what?

MIRREN. Meaning it's your driving that's crap.

ALEX. . . . !

MIRREN. You batter along the road as fast as you can and then screech to a halt as soon as you see anything coming towards you.

ALEX. We're in a hurry.

MIRREN. But there's no point in racing and stopping. You want to go at a comfortable speed. When you see a car coming, all you do is judge how fast they're going, work out where you'll meet and adjust your speed slightly so that you meet at a passing place.

ALEX. Really.

MIRREN. They're passing places. Not stopping places. You shouldn't have to stop. Just slow down a bit.

BRIAN. It's Zen.

MIRREN. You need to learn to adjust.

BRIAN. Zen and the art of single-track roads. Optimising the way you meet other traffic. Minimising the disturbance to either side. Oneness.

MIRREN. Common-sense.

BRIAN. It's that yoga stuff, Alex. Breathing, that's the secret. You need to control it. You need to learn how to breathe.

ALEX. I know how to fucking breathe. I've been doing it for years.

BRIAN. It's just a suggestion.

ALEX. Well, I suggest that unless you want to walk the rest of the way you let me worry about the driving.

MIRREN. That's fair enough, Brian. Let Alex worry.

A beat.

MIRREN. D'you think we've cooled down again yet?

27

On the road.

BRIAN. Left on to the A830. Past Arisaig. Yachting centre. And the sands of Morar. Loch Morar is the deepest in Scotland. Supposed to have a monster too.

ALEX. Mallaig. Another fucking ferry.

BRIAN. Brilliant. Over the sea to Skye.

A beat.

ALEX. Where does she live, your pal?

MIRREN. The other side of those mountains.

ALEX. Christ.

MIRREN. The road goes round them, not over them.

ALEX. Just as well.

MIRREN. Forty-five minutes. An hour at most.

BRIAN. Is she expecting you?

MIRREN. She doesn't expect anything. You'll like her.

28

IONA's *house on Skye.* BRIAN *and* ALEX *poke about.*

BRIAN. Iona's. What a place.

ALEX. Old cottage. Bit run down.

BRIAN. Right on the coast.

ALEX. Wedged between the mountains and the water.

BRIAN. And absolutely full of . . .

ALEX. Mice.

BRIAN. . . . Books.

ALEX. No telly. Lots of rocks.

BRIAN. And the smell. Burning peat.

ALEX. Rising damp.

BRIAN. And Iona . . .

    MIRREN *introduces* IONA.

IONA. Hi!

ALEX. You're American!

IONA. Canadian.

ALEX. Oh.

IONA. Is that a problem?

ALEX. No. It's just . . . I wasn't expecting . . . that's all.

BRIAN. We were just saying what a nice place.

IONA. Thanks.

BRIAN. All these books.

MIRREN. Brian likes books.

IONA. Me too.

BRIAN. Good.

ALEX. Great.

    Pause.

ALEX. Mirren said you might be able to help us with the car.

IONA. Not me. Serge, my partner. He's the one you want.

ALEX. Right. Serge.

IONA. He's French. In case you weren't . . . expecting . . .

ALEX. No. I . . . well . . .

IONA. He's not here though. He's in Ullapool.They're having
a ceilidh tomorrow night. He helps them with the P.A. He's
very . . . practical.

ALEX. Ah. That's not much good for us, though.

    Pause.

MIRREN. Iona says you can stay here and then go over to
Ullapool tomorrow. If you want.

ALEX. We should press on.

MIRREN. You've got no lights. You'll not get very far before
dark.

IONA. You can travel in daylight tomorrow. And I'm sure Serge will be able to help.

BRIAN. You're sure it's not a problem?

IONA. Not at all.

BRIAN. It's very kind of you.

MIRREN. We could give Iona a lift tomorrow as well.

ALEX. We?

IONA. I haven't been to a ceilidh for months. What d'you say?

BRIAN. Alex?

IONA. I'll cook you dinner . . .

   Pause.

ALEX. Yeah. Why not. We're in no hurry anyway, are we!

BRIAN. He's been doing all the driving. He's a bit stressed.

IONA. I've got just the thing for loosening those shoulders.

ALEX. What would that be?

IONA. A gorgeous fifteen-year old . . .

29

IONA'*s house. Later. The four are sprawled. Food has been eaten. Whisky is being drunk.*

BRIAN. It's one of those whiskies where you can't pronounce its name till you're on your fourth glass.

ALEX. You sound pretty fluent.

BRIAN. Lovely meal.

IONA. Thanks.

MIRREN. It was delicious.

IONA. An old family recipe. From back home.

   Pause.

BRIAN. How did you end up here, Iona? From Canada?

IONA. I used to work in the oil industry. Came out to Aberdeen. Spent some time on the rigs then decided I wanted to write.

BRIAN. But why Skye?

IONA. It was the geology first. It's amazing. It's like a crossroads of different rock types and periods. Those mountains are the collision of two different eras. We're right on the edge of the European plate and it's grinding against and buckling under the pressure of the plate moving in under the Atlantic. Like two sides in a war that lasts for millions of years. And this is the front line.

BRIAN. Is that what you're writing about?

IONA. Partly . . .

MIRREN. Makes you a war correspondent.

BRIAN. Geology's answer to Kate Adie!

They laugh.

MIRREN. Alex thinks it's all just rocks.

IONA. It is. But some rocks are very interesting.

ALEX. You're here because of our interesting rocks.

IONA. There's other things too.

ALEX. Like what?

IONA. The people. The quality of life. And because it's so beautiful.

ALEX. Oh.

IONA. Have you been here before?

ALEX. No.

IONA. Wouldn't you say it's beautiful?

ALEX. I suppose it's alright.

IONA. Alright!

ALEX. It's very nice.

IONA. Nice! It's beautiful. Why don't you admit it?

ALEX. I just did.

IONA. You said it was 'nice'.

ALEX. Same thing.

IONA. No way. It's beautiful.

ALEX. Fine. It is.

IONA. So why not say so?

ALEX. Because . . .

IONA. Because?

ALEX. I can't.

IONA. Can't what?

ALEX. Can't say it. Okay? When you say it, it sounds fine. When I say it, it sounds . . . wrong.

A beat.

MIRREN. How can it sound wrong?

ALEX. It just does.

IONA. That's crazy.

ALEX. It's one of those words.

MIRREN. Say it.

ALEX. No.

MIRREN. Go on.

ALEX. I can't. I can think it but I can't say it. It's just . . . It's not part of my language, alright?

MIRREN. It's not much of a language if you can't say that.

ALEX. Well, it's the only one I've got.

Pause.

IONA. Brian, what's he talking about?

BRIAN. Eskimos and snow.

IONA. Inuit.

BRIAN. Whatever. The thing is they've got seventeen words for snow, haven't they. But no word for . . . forest. Or something like that. 'Cause they don't need one, do they?

ALEX. You're pissed.

IONA. We're all pissed.

ALEX. Eskimos and snow?

IONA. Inuit.

MIRREN. Are you serious, Brian?

BRIAN. See where we live, right? Seventeen words for dogshit.

ALEX. Rubbish.

BRIAN. It's not.

IONA. Can you say it?

BRIAN. I can say anything when I'm drunk. Especially when I'm drunk on such beautiful whisky after such a beautiful meal with such beautiful company.

BRIAN *and* IONA *fall into giggling.*

ALEX. I think he's had enough.

MIRREN. He's not the only one, is he.

ALEX *and* MIRREN *catch each other's eye. A beat.*

ALEX. Where are we sleeping?

IONA. Oh. You two are in here. There's stuff over there.

ALEX. Thanks.

BRIAN. But it's still early.

ALEX. It's late. Very late.

MIRREN. Yeah. Maybe it is.

MIRREN *gets up to go.* IONA *follows suit.*

MIRREN. I'll say goodnight.

IONA. Oh well. Me too, then.

BRIAN. Night.

They exit.

BRIAN. What's up with you?

ALEX. What d'you mean?

BRIAN. We were having a nice time.

ALEX. You were.

BRIAN. Relax.

ALEX. I can't. I'm scared. I'm scared I'm going to have blunt instruments applied to all my joints. That's not something that's easily pushed to the back of the mind.

BRIAN. Binks isn't going to find us here, is he. Make the most of it. I mean, I didn't ask to be dragged into this but at least I'm going with it.

ALEX. I didn't drag you into this.

BRIAN. You did. You always do.

ALEX. You didn't have to come.

BRIAN. You wouldn't have found your way past Uddingston.

ALEX. Oh, right. 'Cause you're Mister Encyclopedia-fucking-Brittanica and I'm just a stupid bastard?

BRIAN. Shite.

ALEX. How come I got the job then, eh? How come nobody would take on the great brain?

BRIAN. Fuck off.

ALEX. If your brother had a decent capitalist car instead of that heap of communist junk, that's exactly what I would do. I'd phone for a taxi; if there was a taxi. Or a phone.

BRIAN. Well there's not so why don't you just shut up and go to sleep?

ALEX. Don't give me that shit.

BRIAN. Where are you going?

ALEX. I'm not sleeping here. It's like the fucking Waltons.

BRIAN. Too beautiful for you?

ALEX. Hey how about seventeen different words for 'fuck you'. Fucking eskimos.

BRIAN. Inuit.

ALEX. Fuck off.

ALEX *leaves.*

30

Next morning. ALEX *is hung-over.*

ALEX. I felt bad the next day. My neck was really stiff from curling up in the back seat and my head was throbbing from the whisky. I was cold and I felt a bit sick as well. Not a good start.

Anyway, I struggle out of the car and it's dead early but I can't sleep anymore 'cause the sun's up. Not that it's warm mind – fuck no. Just too bright. So I need to have a piss and I wander down to the rocks by the shore – I'm not wanting to go back into the house, just yet – and I have one of those orgasmic early morning slashes that seem to go on for hours and I start to feel a bit better. I decide a bit of sea breeze might clear my head and I clamber up a big bastard of a rock towards the sound of the waves. And I'm up there looking out.

There's rocks, then a bit of beach, then more rocks and then cliffs. There's huge seagulls swooping about and the sea looks chilly but kind of quiet – like it hasn't had to get up yet. And then there's this seal. I can see its head bobbing in the water. I thought it might be an otter at first but it's too big so it has to be a seal. It's not really that close – it's over by the sandy bit and I'm still up on this big rock – but I've never seen a real seal before except in the zoo so it's close enough for me to sit there and watch it bobbing about and ducking under and coming back up again. And I'm kind of enjoying it. It feels like a secret. It feels special. It feels warmer. Then it all fucks up.

It comes in closer to the beach and it starts to look a bit weird. A bit un-fucking-seal-like. Suspiciously fucking human, in fact. And it comes even closer to the beach and it stands up. And the head is connected to a body, with arms and legs and it's walking out of the water and it's her. Mirren. Wading out of the fucking sea like Ursula Andress in Dr No. Except she doesn't have the knife, or the shell, or the fucking bikini.

And I'm watching her and not feeling a bit like big Sean. 'Cause I'm freezing. My jacket's too thin. My feet are wet. And my trainers don't have any grip on slippery rock. I'm the wrong person. In the wrong place. And if this beach had bouncers I'd never be allowed in. But she's down there, hair drying in the wind. The Queen of the club. And I hate her. Because there's a word for it. There's a word. And I'm thinking it. I'm thinking it. But I can't fucking say it.

31

In the car. On the road to Ullapool.

ALEX. The Skye Bridge.

BRIAN. Opened October 1995. Highest toll in Europe.

ALEX. A87.

BRIAN. Eilean Donan Castle. The view that launched a thousand shortbread tins. Only built eighty years ago.

ALEX. Left on to the A890.

BRIAN. Loch Carron.

ALEX. Left again onto the A896.

BRIAN. Loch Kishorn. They used to build oil platforms there. Abandoned now.

ALEX. The Bonnie Concrete Banks.

BRIAN. Shieldaig. Torridon. Kinlochewe.

ALEX. Loch Maree.

BRIAN. Thirteen miles long with twenty-four islands.

ALEX. Gairloch.

BRIAN. Trout fishing and a nine-hole golf course.

ALEX. Inverewe.

BRIAN. Famous house and gardens.

ALEX. Aultbea?

BRIAN. Uhm . . . nothing . . . except . . .

ALEX. Fucking hell!

BRIAN. A very steep descent.

32

Gruinard Bay. A stop for water. MIRREN *and* ALEX *wait for the others to return.*

MIRREN. Brian seemed pretty keen to go for the water.

ALEX. Yeah.

MIRREN. Did you two have a fight last night?

ALEX. Sort of.

MIRREN. About what?

ALEX. He thought I should be nicer to you and Iona.

MIRREN. What did you say?

ALEX. I said I'd think about it.

MIRREN. Really?

ALEX. No. I told him to fuck off.

   MIRREN *smiles.*

ALEX. He thinks I worry too much.

MIRREN. What do you think?

ALEX. It's not planned this, y'know. I don't really know what we're doing here. I'm just making it up as I go.

MIRREN. Thrown in at the deep-end. You've done all right so far.

ALEX. Yeah. But what's next?

MIRREN. S'no reason to worry.

ALEX. No?

MIRREN. There's nothing you can do. Just accept it.

ALEX. And relax?

MIRREN. One thing at a time. Try just accepting first.

ALEX. How am I supposed to do that?

MIRREN. You need to learn how to breathe.

ALEX. Are you taking the piss?

MIRREN. Aye.

Pause.

ALEX. Look, last night . . . I didn't mean to be . . . you know . . .

MIRREN. I know.

ALEX. It's just that . . .

MIRREN. What?

ALEX. Well. Up here. Like this. I feel a bit . . . as if . . . I mean, I feel like . . .

IONA *and* BRIAN *return with water for the car.*

BRIAN. Hey. You see that island over there. Iona was telling me the government tested chemical weapons on it during the war. They infected it with anthrax and no-one could go on it till a few years ago when they finally cleaned it up. Isn't that wild?

ALEX. Yeah. Wild.

IONA. We got the water. We can get going again.

ALEX. No rush.

BRIAN. You've changed your tune.

MIRREN. He's learning how to breathe.

IONA. Getting in touch with nature, eh Alex?

ALEX. Not exactly.

IONA. Didn't you go bird-watching this morning too?

ALEX. Eh?

IONA. I'm sure I saw you from the kitchen. See anything interesting?

ALEX. No. Not really. I mean, I wasn't looking.

A beat.

Maybe we should get going.

BRIAN. Thought we weren't in a rush.

MIRREN. My Granny always said things would get done faster if everyone just slowed down a wee bit.

BRIAN. My Granny was like that. 'Remember son, the world's your oxter.'

IONA. I don't get it.

33

BINKS *stops on the road to Inverness.*

BINKS. Drumna-fucking-drochit? What kinda name is that?

A SMALL BOY *enters licking an ice lolly.* BINKS *and he eye each other warily.* BINKS *covets the lolly.*

BOY. Are you going to the exhibition? I am.

BINKS. What exhibition?

BOY. The official Loch Ness Monster Exhibition. Over there. Are you going?

BINKS. Naw. Give us a bit of your lolly?

BOY. Naw.

Pause. BINKS *schemes.*

BINKS. I'll tell you a secret if you give us a bit.

BOY *shakes his head.*

BINKS. Two secrets then. For one wee sook.

BOY *swithers.*

BINKS. Three secrets. One lick.

BOY *succombs and hands over the lolly.*

BOY. Tell me the secrets then.

BINKS. First. Nessie doesnae exist.

The BOY *is crestfallen.* BINKS *sucks on the lolly.*

BINKS. Second. Neither does Santa.

The BOY *is shocked.*

BINKS. Oh aye and third. I'm keeping this.

The BOY *bursts into tears and runs off.* BINKS *enjoys the lolly, pleased with himself.*

BINKS. Eh? . . . Aye, Ronnie son. It's true.

Candy from a baby!

He laughs.

34

Arriving in Ullapool.

ALEX. You come into Ullapool along Loch Broom. It's full of big fishing boats from all over the place. Tied up in rows. Backing out towards the sea. Like a procession.

BRIAN. Established by the British Fisheries Association in 1788.

ALEX. And as pretty as a trawler.

BRIAN. It does look a bit dull.

ALEX. Or it did until we pulled up outside the community hall . . .

BRIAN. . . . and met Serge!

SERGE *emerges like Eric Cantona dressed by Salvador Dali.*

SERGE. Na-na! What are you doing here?

IONA. Thought I'd come to the party.

SERGE. And Mirren! Mon dieu. What a surprise!

MIRREN. How's things?

SERGE. Ça va. You know. Much better now that you are here.

MIRREN. These are some friends of mine. Brian. And Alex.

This is Serge . . .

ALEX. We guessed.

SERGE. So, you are all here for the ceilidh, yes.

MIRREN. Not exactly. We're heading north but we're having some trouble with the car . . .

SERGE. Ah. The Riva. A classic.

He pats the car affectionately.

SERGE. Let me guess. Alternator?

ALEX. And the radiator.

SERGE. Ah. Cooling system and the electrical? Serious. But not fatal, I think. You have come how far?

BRIAN. From Motherwell. Near Glasgow.

SERGE. In this! Then you are officially Heroes of the State. Mad, but heroic.

ALEX. Iona thought you might be able to help.

SERGE. Certainly, but I must first help with the ceilidh. There's so much to do and so little time.

MIRREN. Later maybe?

SERGE. Certainly. Later. But you will stay? You dance, you sing, you sleep. And tomorrow you leave in a healthier car, yes?

ALEX. Tomorrow?

IONA. Go on.

BRIAN. We haven't anywhere to stay.

SERGE. Pas de problème. The hall, I sleep in a back room. It is big enough. Mirren?

MIRREN. It's not up to me. Alex?

Pause.

ALEX. Fine.

SERGE. Bon. Maintenant. Does anyone know something about microphones?

BRIAN. Well, actually . . .

ALEX. Brian knows something about everything.

MIRREN. Yeah. He's your man.

SERGE. Excellent.

He begins steering BRIAN *into the hall.*

BRIAN. It's only been karaoke I've helped out at before . . .

SERGE. Karaoke. Ceilidh. The same. Wan singer wan song, no?

35

The ceilidh.

ALEX. The ceilidh was mad. Really weird. The place was full of folk from the village. And fishermen and crofters and some tourists and . . . us. And it was a mix. A huge mix. They mixed the music and they mixed the people and they mixed the fucking drink and it was . . . just a bit much. That's all. Just a bit too much.

ALEX *is in the car park outside the hall.* IONA *comes out to join him.*

IONA. Hi. You okay out here?

ALEX. Fine.

IONA. What are you doing?

ALEX. Practising breathing. It's hot in there.

IONA. Having a good time, though?

ALEX. It's not quite what I expected.

IONA. How so?

ALEX. It seems strange coming to a ceilidh and hearing some highlander belt out 'Folsom Prison Blues'.

IONA. What would you prefer?

ALEX. I don't know.

IONA. Something in Gaelic, maybe?

ALEX. Yeah. Maybe.

IONA *begins to sing, in perfect Gaelic, a lament.* ALEX *listens in some astonishment. She finishes.*

ALEX. I didn't know . . . You never said. That was amazing.

IONA. You didn't understand a word though did you?

ALEX. No.

IONA. But you got every single syllable of Johnny Cash.

ALEX. So?

IONA. So why does it matter what anybody does for their party piece?

ALEX. It's complicated. I suppose I thought people up here would be less . . . confused.

IONA. Confused? About what?

ALEX. Who they are.

IONA. Who's confused? Look. See that?

ALEX. What?

IONA. Satellite dish. We're not cut off from the outside world.

ALEX. I know that.

IONA. You think we should be like a big Braveheart theme park? Pickled in tradition? C'mon Alex. Loosen up. You can have it all.

ALEX. How?

IONA. Choose your influences . . .

ALEX. I'm not sure you get to choose . . .

Pause.

IONA. What are you looking for?

ALEX. Just . . . somewhere that doesn't make me feel like an outsider.

IONA. Or someone.

ALEX. . . .

A beat. MIRREN *emerges and comes to join them.*

MIRREN. God, it's hot in there. What are you two up to?

IONA. Just chewing the fat.

Pause.

IONA. Saw you dancing with Brian.

MIRREN. Yeah.

ALEX. Any broken toes?

MIRREN. I think I got off lightly.

IONA. What's he up to now?

MIRREN. He's with the Ukranians. From the factory ship.

ALEX. I didn't realise they were Ukranian.

IONA. They've been anchored in the loch for months. No fuel and no money to buy any. Their government was supposed to send it but they seem to've forgotten. Their ship's just rusting away.

ALEX. What are they doing with Brian?

MIRREN. He's reciting Burns. One of them is translating. They're big fans apparently.

ALEX. I didn't know he knew any Burns.

From inside sound of a woman starting to sing a slow ballad.

MIRREN. Oh. I love this song. Come and dance.

IONA. Not me girl. I'm done. Alex'll give you a birl, though. Eh?

ALEX. I'm not exactly Fred Astaire.

IONA. No, but you're not Fred Flintstone either. Go on.

MIRREN. Well?

ALEX. Here?

MIRREN. It's cooler.

ALEX *and* MIRREN *start to dance tentatively.*

IONA. Jeez Alex, it's not basketball. You're allowed contact.

MIRREN. You're trying too hard. Just let it happen.

ALEX *relaxes.*

IONA. That's better. See you later.

IONA *exits.*

ALEX. You're pretty good.

MIRREN. I used to go to classes. When I was wee. You're not too bad . . . once you relax.

ALEX. It'll be all that breathing.

MIRREN. You ought to do it more often.

ALEX. Breathe?

MIRREN. Relax.

ALEX. I'll try.

MIRREN. Don't try, just . . .

ALEX. . . . let it happen.

Pause.

MIRREN. What are you going to do when you get to Thurso?

ALEX. Try and sell the board.

MIRREN. And then?

ALEX. Depends.

MIRREN. On what?

ALEX. Lots of things.

MIRREN. You're not going home.

ALEX. Can't. Not for a while.

MIRREN. Haven't you got family?

ALEX. They won't miss me.

MIRREN. What about Brian?

ALEX. His dad probably hasn't even noticed that he's gone yet.

Pause. Song finishes.

MIRREN. I know some people in Thurso. Surfers. I might be able to help you find a buyer.

ALEX. That'd be good.

MIRREN. There's one guy I could introduce you to. He knows everybody.

ALEX. You're going to come with us to Thurso?

MIRREN. If that's all right?

ALEX. What about Tongue?

MIRREN. I just need to pick a few things up. Flying visit.

ALEX. But this guy . . . Tom? Won't he mind?

MIRREN. That's my problem.

ALEX. Who is he?

MIRREN. He's someone who thinks I've fucked my life up and is determined to save me from myself. I embarrass him. He harasses me. It's a long story.

ALEX. So . . . How d'you know him then?

MIRREN. He's my father.

ALEX. Oh.

Pause.

MIRREN. You surprised?

ALEX. A bit.

MIRREN. Doesn't just happen in Motherwell you know.

ALEX. No. It's not that. I . . .

MIRREN. . . . ?

ALEX. I better go and see how Brian's doing.

MIRREN. Oh.

ALEX. And Serge. He might've forgotten.

MIRREN. Try the bar.

ALEX. Okay. Thanks.

He exits.

36

Inverness. BINKS *has a new pal* GUNN. *They are pissed.*

GUNN. No. No. No. Definitely not. I'm telling you. Absolutely.
Under no circumstances. I am quite certain. No.

Pause.

BINKS. Are you sure?

GUNN *belches.*

GUNN. I could be wrong.

BINKS. Christ man!

GUNN. Wait now. Just let me think . . . They had a ladder you
said.

BINKS. That's right.

GUNN. Tied to the roof?

BINKS. Eh?

GUNN. And what kind of car was it?

BINKS. A Lada.

GUNN. I know about that.

BINKS. Well, why are you asking?

GUNN. I need to know about the car.

BINKS. It had a surf-board tied to the roof.

GUNN. As well as the ladder?

BINKS. On top of the Lada! A surf-board on top of a Lada.

GUNN. Well, I'm sure I would've noticed that. That's not
something you see every day, is it. I'm sure I would've noticed.

BINKS. But you didn't.

GUNN. Didn't what?

BINKS. You didn't notice it.

GUNN. Did I not?

BINKS *growls and grabs* GUNN *by the lapels.*

BINKS. You were working. On the roadworks. On the bridge over
the Beauly Firth. Right?

GUNN. Right.

BINKS. And you did not see a Lada with a surf-board on top,
crossing the bridge. Right?

GUNN. Right.

BINKS. Right!

> *Pause.* BINKS *releases his grip.*

GUNN. Are you sure you don't know what kind of car it was? Must've been awful over-loaded . . .

> BINKS' *patience snaps. He produces a knife.*

GUNN. Are we going for a kebab then?

BINKS. Aye. Oh aye.

37

The dregs of the ceilidh.

IONA. Time gentlemen please!

> *Groans and shuffling as people leave.*

MIRREN. Serge, what about the car?

SERGE. Ah. Okay. I remember. I will look at it now. Give me the keys.

ALEX. But it's four in the morning?

SERGE. So?

ALEX. Aren't you tired?

SERGE. I am wide awake.

ALEX. Are you on something?

SERGE. Alex. Too many questions. I am fine. Hunky dory. Trust me. Give me the keys.

> ALEX *reluctantly hands them over.*

SERGE. You will go to sleep. You will have wonderful dreams. When you wake up your car will be transformed.

ALEX. Be careful with it.

SERGE. I will be gentle. I am French.

> *He leaves to attend to the car.* ALEX *is still concerned.*

IONA. It's all right, Alex. He knows what he's doing.

ALEX. Where exactly did he train?

IONA. Nice.

ALEX. Technical college?

IONA. School of Art.

ALEX. Sorry?

IONA. Didn't I say? He's a sculptor.

ALEX. A sculptor?

IONA. But he does do a lot of work with Ladas and Skodas and things.

ALEX. What kind of work?

IONA. Well, normally he cuts them in half and welds wings on to them. Angel-type wings. Or legs. Sometimes it's legs.

A beat.

MIRREN. Alex? Are you all right?

ALEX. Yeah. I'm going to go to sleep and have wonderful dreams and wake up to find the car transformed. Fine.

MIRREN. Are you sure?

ALEX. Just letting it happen . . .

BRIAN spirals over to them very drunk.

BRIAN. Chudovyj! *(*TCHU-*daw-vey)*

He has acquired a Ukranian word.

ALEX. Yeah. Chudovyj. Very good.

BRIAN. It is. Say it. Chudovyj. Go on.

ALEX. Chudovyj.

BRIAN. Perfect.

They are all now heading off to the back room.

BRIAN. Chudovyj! Doesn't it sound good?

ALEX. Yeah. But what does it mean?

BRIAN. It's Ukranian for 'beautiful'.

They exit.

Interval.

38

Next morning. SERGE *musters the still sleepy travellers to the unveiling of the car.*

SERGE. Good morning Comrades. You must prepare to witness a transfiguration.

MIRREN. Have you been up all night?

SERGE. I have been creating.

ALEX. But have you fixed the car?

SERGE. So basic! The leaking radiator leaks no more. The alternator is still weak but the battery strong again.

BRIAN. What about the lights?

SERGE. You have no lights. You must be guided by the brightness of your imagination.

BRIAN. Oh.

ALEX. Fuck.

SERGE. Do not worry. The car will carry you where you need it to. I have refreshed its spirit.

ALEX. You've changed the oil?

SERGE. I have changed the car.

ALEX. How, exactly?

BRIAN. Serge . . .

SERGE. The car was unhappy. I asked it why. Then I made it happier.

BRIAN. You asked it why?

ALEX. What was it you took last night?

BRIAN. What did it say?

SERGE. It was unhappy because it was brown. Not even a golden sun-tanned brown but a dark, horrible brown like . . .

ALEX. Shit.

SERGE. Exactly. The car was unhappy because it was the colour of shit. Merde.

ALEX. Oh God.

SERGE. So I cured it . . . Et voilà!

He removes the dustsheet. The Lada is now practically fluorescent with day-glo colours. There is a shocked silence.

SERGE. You have a car with a smile on its face.

MIRREN. Oh no.

ALEX. Fucking hell.

IONA. Serge . . .

SERGE. What is the matter? Don't you like it?

ALEX. It's . . . It's . . .

SERGE. Bright?

ALEX. Mmm.

SERGE. Camouflage for you.

ALEX. Camouflage!

SERGE. You blend in by standing out. You look truly like surfers now. Not robbers skulking around the Highlands.

MIRREN. Certainly going to be difficult to skulk in that.

ALEX. Brian, are you all right?

BRIAN *has become catatonic with shock.*

MIRREN. Brian? Say something.

There is no response.

IONA. What's wrong with him?

ALEX. I think he's in shock. I've seen it before.

MIRREN. He's been like this before?

ALEX. When his Mum unplugged his computer to hoover his bedroom and crashed a programme he'd been working on for months.

MIRREN. How long was he like this?

ALEX. Well . . .

IONA. Couple of minutes?

MIRREN. An hour?

ALEX. Three days.

MIRREN. What!

ALEX. It's alright. This probably won't be as long.

MIRREN. What do we do?

ALEX. We might as well get going. He'll come out of it when he's ready.

IONA. Are you sure you'll be alright?

ALEX. Any better ideas?

They guide BRIAN *carefully towards the car. He is reluctant to go anywhere near it. They coax him into the back seat and prepare to set off.*

SERGE. The muses shall protect you. You are travelling in a work of art.

ALEX. Well, at least it doesn't have wings.

39

On the road. In the car. BRIAN *in the back.* ALEX *and* MIRREN *in front.* BRIAN *talks directly to the audience.*

BRIAN. I'd been working on it for nearly twelve weeks. It was basically a database with some tricks built in. Horse racing. I had information on over three hundred horses. All kinds of information. It was just getting to the point where the predictions were reliable. The point where I could start to make money.

ALEX. A835. North out of Ullapool.

MIRREN. There's a wee road that turns off at Drumrunie. Goes round the coast to Lochinver. It's a bit of a detour though.

ALEX. What do think Brian? Turn off or carry on? Eh? Brian?

BRIAN. I'd only went to the toilet. Two minutes. I was sitting there working out how much cash I could get together to stake when I heard the hoover. It came to me quite slowly where the sound was coming from. I waited until it stopped before I could bear to go see.

MIRREN. ' . . . a wild and adventurous road with magnificent scenery . . . ' That's what it says. In your book. Look.

BRIAN. She was just plugging it back in when I got there. She switched it on and smiled at me. 'That's the place a wee bit cleaner anyway.' I was looking at the screen. It was more than just a wee bit cleaner. It was blank. I saw all that information, all those facts and figures, all swirling around and down into the big black hole of my mum's hoover bag. I saw her sucking them off the screen and out from between the keys with her handy hose attachment. Nozzling it all into oblivion.

ALEX. Will we turn off then, Brian? You're the navigator. That a
no then? Straight on, d'you think?

MIRREN. I suppose it's not so important to avoid the main roads
now.

ALEX. Now that we're camouflaged.

BRIAN. She died three months after that. We all stood at the
grave chucking dirt down on top of the coffin. Me and George
and my Dad. My shoes were leaking and I thought about the
money I could've made with the programme. I had an urge to
jump into the grave and wipe all that dirt off the polished
wood. I wished I had a yellow duster to do the job properly.
But I didn't. So my mum disappeared into a black hole too.

ALEX. Look at the mountains, Brian. They're incredible.

MIRREN. Suilven. Canisp. Ben More Assynt.

ALEX. Ever heard of them? Anything interesting ever happen
here?

MIRREN. It says here that they 'seem as if they have tumbled
down from the clouds, having nothing to do with the country or
each other in shape, material, position or character, and look
very much as if they were wondering how they got there.'

ALEX. Hey Brian, that's us, eh? Nothing to do with anything and
wondering how we got here. That's us.

BRIAN. George joined the army. My dad hit the bottle. He sold
the computer to pay an electricity bill. I started spending a lot
of time at the library. Nothing got better. Everything just
seemed to get worse. I wondered how bad it could get before it
would all stop.

ALEX. What?

BRIAN. Stop.

ALEX. Why?

BRIAN. I need some air.

ALEX. Okay. No problem. We'll pull in. Take a wee break.

MIRREN. You're back. Are you all right?

BRIAN. I'm fine. I just need to stretch my legs.

ALEX. All right. Good. Take your time. Take it easy. Remember
to breathe and everything.

BRIAN. I'm fine.

40

At the roadside. BRIAN *wanders away from the other two a bit.*

MIRREN. Do you think he's okay?

ALEX. Yeah. He'll be fine.

MIRREN. Should we go with him?

ALEX. No. Let him get some air.

MIRREN. The car seems better.

ALEX. Serge seems to have done something right.

MIRREN. He's made it happier.

ALEX. Yeah.

    Pause.

ALEX. Where are we?

MIRREN. Assynt. More or less.

ALEX. Nice and quiet. Peaceful.

MIRREN. D'you think?

ALEX. Feels like the middle of nowhere.

MIRREN. D'you know what you're sitting on?

ALEX. A stone.

MIRREN. Gable end of a croft-house.

ALEX. A house?

MIRREN. There's another one over there. And there. Probably another dozen along the glen.

ALEX. Yeah?

MIRREN. Wasn't always so nice and quiet round here.

ALEX. What happened?

MIRREN. Clearances.Whole families packed off to Canada and Australia. Driven out to make room for sheep.

ALEX. Money talks. Nothing changes, eh?

MIRREN. This changed. They changed it into scenery. The Great Wilderness? The Highland Landscape? It's an invention. I don't think it's peaceful. I think it's sad.

ALEX. Where I come from, they took all the jobs away then called it a special development area.

    BRIAN, *unnoticed, has found a stream. He sticks his head under the water and keeps it there.*

MIRREN. Doesn't it piss you off?

ALEX. Lots of things piss me off.

MIRREN. I'd noticed. Me included?

ALEX. Well. You did. A bit.

MIRREN. Why? What did I do?

ALEX. You just fitted in, that's all. Looked like you belonged.
I feel . . . out of place. A misfit.

MIRREN. It's still Scotland. You're Scottish.

ALEX. I'm a foreigner here. Even the midges know that. Look,
my face is like a page of braille. They don't bother you at all.

MIRREN. You think they're picking on you?

ALEX. Insect antibodies. An immune system for repelling
invaders.

MIRREN. Maybe, if you stay still they'll leave you alone.

ALEX. We're not very good at that though, are we. Me and Brian.
We're running.

MIRREN. What is it?

ALEX. Where's he gone? Hey? Brian? . . . BRIAN!

They run across to BRIAN *and pull him out. He shows no
signs of life.* ALEX *shakes him.*

MIRREN. Is he alright?

ALEX. Brian! Talk to me! Say something!

A beat. A cough from BRIAN.

BRIAN. If I'm going to get the kiss of life, I'd rather Mirren did it.

Pause. Then ALEX *starts to hit him.*

ALEX. You stupid bastard.What are you playing at?

MIRREN. Alex. Stop it.

MIRREN *pulls them apart and they calm a little.*

BRIAN. Sorry.

ALEX. Sorry! What were you trying to do?

BRIAN. Drown myself.

A beat.

ALEX. Jesus Christ! It's only a fucking car. It's not even a very
good one.

BRIAN. That's not the point.

ALEX. What is the point?

MIRREN. Brian. It's not the end of the world.

ALEX. It fucking will be if you try that again. I'll kill you myself.

MIRREN. Alex.

ALEX. Is this what you've been cooking up in the car all this way? Is that what was going on? What were you thinking about?

BRIAN. It doesn't matter. I didn't realise you were going to get so worked up about it.

ALEX. Thanks.

Pause.

BRIAN. Can we go back to the car now? I'm wet.

ALEX. Yeah, you fucking are . . .

41

Helmsdale. BINKS *at a garage. Chats to the* PUMP-HAND.

PUMP. There now. That's you full. Ten pounds, please.

BINKS. Christ.

PUMP. Aye, it'll be dearer than you're used to. Still, you're lucky you're just passing through. We have to pay these prices all the time.

BINKS. What a shame.

PUMP. It is. It's alright for you. You're going somewhere, aren't you. Where are you going?

BINKS. Thurso.

PUMP. There see. You're going to Thurso and then you'll be going somewhere else no doubt. Then somewhere else. Am I right?

BINKS. More or less.

PUMP. And is it business or pleasure?

BINKS. Business. As in 'mind your own'.

PUMP. Ah. You must be a salesman. I can tell. What you selling then?

BINKS. Private Health Care.

PUMP. Och I've no need for that myself. Fit as a fiddle.

BINKS. That could change. Very suddenly.

PUMP. Not here. Nope. Last sudden change we had round here was decimalisation.

BINKS. Where is this?

PUMP. Helmsdale.

BINKS. How far's that from Thurso?

PUMP. It varies.Thirty miles. Forty maybe if you go via John O'Groats.

BINKS. John O Groats? Is that near here?

PUMP. Not too far.

BINKS. How do I get there?

PUMP. Ah, you don't want to go there. Nothing to see. A hotel. A woollens shop. A signpost. It's not . . .

BINKS. How do I get there?

PUMP. Well, it's up to you. You'd want to carry on here and go straight through Wick . . . believe me, everyone wants to go straight through Wick . . . and then you can't miss it. Turn left for Thurso once you've seen it.

BINKS. I don't suppose you've seen two guys in a . . .

PUMP. A what?

BINKS. Ach, never mind.

PUMP. Suit yourself.

A beat.

PUMP. Was there something else?

BINKS. I gave you a twenty.

PUMP. Did you?

BINKS. Aye. I did. Give me ma change.

PUMP. Are you sure it was a twenty?

BINKS. Does petrol burn?

BINKS *flips open the lid of a zippo and sparks it into life as he grabs the attendant.*

PUMP. In the name of God! What are you doing? Put it out!

BINKS. Give me ma fucking money before I cremate you.

PUMP. Here take it. Take it all. On the house. Just put that out. PLEASE!

42

On the road. A jet screams past low overhead.

ALEX. What the hell was that?

MIRREN. Jets. Phantoms. They have a base up here. It's a practice area for NATO. Low level flying.

ALEX. God. Any lower and I would've had to pull over to let him pass.

MIRREN. You're getting better, you know.

ALEX. At what?

MIRREN. Passing places. You're using them properly now. It's much better. Eh Brian?

BRIAN. Two steel boxes full of hopes and dreams and fears hurtle towards each other on a narrow road and just as they are about to collide the road widens enough for them to slip past each other with only the lightest of kisses on the cheek. Hello, goodbye, without ever stopping.

Pause.

ALEX. Is that out the Highway Code?

BRIAN. It's life, isn't it.

ALEX. It's only a road, Brian.

BRIAN. The A838. North east from Laxford Bridge. Twenty-five miles to Durness. Then through Sangobeg, all the way round Loch Eriboll, past Portnancon, through Laid then Polla. On to Heilam. The road widens and there it is.

ALEX. What are you on about?

BRIAN. It's on the map, Alex. You can't miss it.

ALEX. Miss what?

BRIAN. The A838. Where it takes you.

ALEX. Thurso?

BRIAN. Before Thurso. Tell him Mirren. Look.

ALEX. Tell me what?

MIRREN. You pass Loch Eriboll and carry on for a bit . . . You come to . . .

BRIAN. Hope.

ALEX. That's stupid.

BRIAN. It's on the map.

MIRREN. It is Alex.

ALEX. I'm surrounded by lunatics. Are we nearly there?

BRIAN. Hope?

ALEX. Tongue!

MIRREN. Not far now.

43

Arriving in Tongue.

ALEX. You come in over a long low bridge that stretches across a kyle of sand and water. The house was on the left before the village itself.

BRIAN. Big grey stone building. Like a manse. A gravel drive and trees.

ALEX. Mirren went to find her dad.

BRIAN. We waited by the car.

ALEX. There was something funny going on with him. I said . . .

BRIAN. 'Are you all right?'

ALEX. And he gave me this look. Like somebody had died.

BRIAN. And he looked worried, so I told him.

ALEX. He told me.

BRIAN. I said . . .

ALEX. 'I'm not going back'.

BRIAN. He says . . .

ALEX. 'What? What d'you mean?'

BRIAN. I said it again.

ALEX. He said it twice.

A beat.

BRIAN. I'm not going back. I can't.

ALEX. But . . .

BRIAN. I've decided.

ALEX. Is this because of the car? Is that what it is?

BRIAN. No.

ALEX. No? What d'you mean, 'no'? You tried to drown yourself.

BRIAN. It's not the car.

ALEX. Well what . . .

BRIAN. I'm not going back. It's because of me. Not you. Not the car. Me. There's no reason now for me to go back there. It's too far behind.

ALEX. Brian, it's a few hours' drive. In a decent car.

BRIAN. It's too far.

Pause.

ALEX. I knew this would happen. You always do this. You always turn something completely simple and straightforward into a big production number. Some fucking defining moment. Some glimpse into the true nature of the fucking universe. Always. Even at school. A hair in your pie and beans and it's a sign from God. Extra custard and it's an omen of plenty. Well, it's not. A hair is a hair. Custard is just custard. They are not fucking karmic telegrams.

Pause.

BRIAN. I'm not going back.

ALEX. We're only here to flog the surf-board and lie low for a bit. It's not supposed to be a turning point in our lives. Nothing's changed. Nothing.

BRIAN. I'm not going back.

ALEX. That's not an argument. That's shite. You're talking shite.

BRIAN. I'm not going.

Pause.

ALEX. What are you going to do?

BRIAN. Don't know.

ALEX. And what am I supposed to do?

BRIAN. Don't know.

ALEX. Brilliant.

BRIAN. I'm not going back.

Pause.

ALEX. Maybe I should've just let you drown.

44

In TOM*'s house. The atmosphere is a bit strained.*

TOM. I could've made something really special. I don't often get the chance, you know.

MIRREN. We can't stay, dad.

TOM. What about it boys? Can't your business wait till tomorrow? I've got venison in the freezer. Have you ever had venison?

ALEX. We really have to be in Thurso tonight.

MIRREN. Before it gets dark.

ALEX. Maybe some other time.

TOM. Yeah well. I suppose if you're a parent these days you live on the crumbs from your children's table.

MIRREN. Dad.

TOM. Where is it this time?

MIRREN. Don't know. Scandinavia, maybe.

TOM. Got anything lined up?

MIRREN. No.

TOM. What a surprise. I'll give you a name of a guy I used to correspond with at the university in Stockholm.

MIRREN. There's no need.

TOM. He'll help you out.

MIRREN. I'll be fine.

TOM. Doing what? Waiting tables? Washing dishes?

MIRREN. Whatever.

TOM. Right. And after Scandanavia?

MIRREN. I don't know.

TOM. No long term plan.

MIRREN. Not really.

TOM. No. I didn't think so.

MIRREN. Dad. Don't start.

Pause.

MIRREN. Show Brian your office. He'll be interested in all that stuff.

TOM. Nice that someone is.

MIRREN. We can clear up.

ALEX. Yeah.

TOM. C'mon then, Brian. I'll show you the electric croft.

BRIAN. Great.

45

BRIAN *and* TOM *go to the office.* MIRREN *and* ALEX *wash up in the kitchen. The scene jumps between the two.*

ALEX. He seems alright.

MIRREN. He thinks I'm wasting my life.

ALEX. At least he worries about you.

MIRREN. I don't want him to.

ALEX. It's his job.

TOM. First class honours, you know. Maths and computer science. Could go anywhere with that. Anywhere. Without having to wash dishes.

BRIAN. She never mentioned it.

TOM. No. She usually doesn't. Makes her seem too much like me.

ALEX. You sure you don't want to hang around longer?

MIRREN. It's not worth it. Things tend to get ugly after a while.

ALEX. You're fidgeting.

MIRREN. This place. Him. It makes me restless. What's so funny?

ALEX. Everywhere we've been so far, you seemed so at home. But now you are home . . . !

MIRREN. This isn't home. We moved here when I was thirteen. I left when I was seventeen. I've not really lived here since.

ALEX. So where's home then?

She shrugs.

TOM. We came up here when Mirren's mother died. I needed a change.

BRIAN. Did you bring all this with you?

TOM. No. Got it when I decided to stay.

BRIAN. It's a lot of stuff.

TOM. Nothing special. PC. Printer. Modem.

BRIAN. Haven't you got a sattelite dish too?

TOM. Aye, but that's just for the football really.

ALEX. So who's the guy you're taking us to see in Thurso? Your uncle? A second-cousin?

MIRREN. A friend. He's difficult to describe.

ALEX. A lot of your friends are!

MIRREN. He's part of the surfing scene.

ALEX. D'you think we will be able to get rid of the board?

MIRREN. He'll be able to tell you. He's a shaper.

ALEX. What's that?

MIRREN. He builds boards. Shapes them. It's very specialised. A real art.

ALEX. So he's well in with the surfers?

MIRREN. Oh yeah. He's like a guru. Kind of . . . mystic.

ALEX. A mystic surf-guru. Can't wait.

BRIAN. And you work from here now?

TOM. Freelance. Do a lot of stuff for software designers in Silicon Valley.

BRIAN. America? From here?

TOM. It's easy enough. I can phone. Fax. E-mail. I can link the machine straight through. Video conference if we need too. It's no problem.

BRIAN. You don't need to go over there at all?

TOM. I go about twice a year. Just for the sunshine. Who'd be a commuter, eh?

BRIAN. I wouldn't know.

MIRREN. You can't make him go back. It's up to him.

ALEX. He doesn't know what he's doing.

MIRREN. Maybe he does.

ALEX. It wasn't meant to be like this. It was only temporary.

MIRREN. Temporary can be a very long time.

TOM. Portable skills. That's the key. You can take them anywhere. Especially now, with all this stuff.

BRIAN. What if you haven't got any skills?

TOM. Everybody's got them. You just have to bring them out.

BRIAN. How?

TOM. You can learn, can't you?

MIRREN. That's what travelling's all about. Change.

ALEX. Aye. But with Brian it's usually just change for the bus.

MIRREN. Not this time.

ALEX. But it's just a trip.

MIRREN. A long trip.

ALEX. Tell me about it.

MIRREN. You've changed too.

ALEX. But I'm not burning my bridges.

MIRREN. Not yet.

TOM. You're thinking about sticking around up here?

BRIAN. If I can. Somewhere.

TOM. There's a lot going on, you know. I'm sure if you'll find
    something. If you look hard enough.

BRIAN. I hope so.

MIRREN. I think you're scared.

ALEX. Of what?

MIRREN. Being alone. You need him. He looks after you.

ALEX. You think so?

MIRREN. Yeah.

ALEX. What about you, then?

MIRREN. I look after myself.

ALEX. You don't need anyone?

MIRREN. No.

ALEX. And you're never scared?

MIRREN. I've been on my own for a long time.

ALEX. That wasn't the question.

TOM. I just want to know that she's alright, that's all. I know she
    thinks I interfere but I just want her to be happy. Is she? D'you
    think she's happy?

BRIAN. I don't know. She seems okay. Maybe you should ask her.

TOM. She won't tell me. I'd be the last to know anything.

BRIAN. I'm sure she's fine.

ALEX. You going to make your goodbyes? We ought to get going before it's too dark.

MIRREN. It won't take long. I've had enough practice.

46

John O'Groats. Bleak. BINKS hovers by a sign-post.

BINKS. Well Ronnie, here we are. John O'Groats. Who'd've thought, eh? The end of the line . . . Aye. I know. Alright. Nearly the end of the line, then . . . Aye. A bit grim is not wrong.

A LADY WALKER clumps up to him in heavy boots.

WALKER. Hello there.

BINKS. . . .

WALKER. I've walked here. All the way.

BINKS. . . .

WALKER. From Land's End, I mean. I've walked all the way.

BINKS. Why?

Pause.

WALKER. Will you take my photograph?

BINKS. I havnae got a camera.

WALKER. With mine. Here. Would you? Go on.

He takes the camera. He takes the picture.

WALKER. Fabulous. No-one would've believed me otherwise. I've got Lands End to John O'Groats all on one film now. And there's still one shot left. Shall I take you?

BINKS. I told you I havnae got a camera.

WALKER. I mean with this. I've one left. I could send it to you.

BINKS. I don't think so.

WALKER. Oh go on. You've come all this way. You might not get another chance. Don't you want something to remember it by?

BINKS. I'm not bothered.

WALKER. It's no trouble. Go on.

BINKS. I don't want my photo taken.

WALKER. I need to use it up anyway.

BINKS. I told you, I . . .

She takes the picture.

WALKER. There. That didn't hurt did it. Would've been nicer if you'd smiled though. Your face won't crack you know.

BINKS *moves towards her. Smiling.*

WALKER. There. See. You've got a lovely smile. Now if you just give me your name and address I can send it to you when I get it developed.

BINKS. Fuck . . .

WALKER. Is that German?

BINKS. . . . You!

BINKS *grabs her camera. She looks up and is dumb with terror. He opens the camera and pulls out the film. She whimpers slightly as he wraps it round and round her head.*

BINKS. I told her, Ronnie. I told her twice.

A gargling noise as the walker is strangled.

I don't want my fucking photo took.

47

On the road to Thurso. Back in the car.

BRIAN. A strange thing happens on the road between Tongue and Thurso. You move from Sutherland into Caithness and suddenly . . .

ALEX. All the scenery disappears.

BRIAN. You move from mountains into flat peat bogs.

ALEX. The flow country.

BRIAN. So it feels like you're back in the Central Belt again.

ALEX. On the road to . . . Shotts.

BRIAN. Then there's Dounreay.

ALEX. Radioactive dustbin.

BRIAN. Prototype Fast Breeder Reactor. Doubled Thurso's population.

ALEX. More physicists than fishermen.

BRIAN. Till they shut it.

ALEX. And then, finally . . .

BRIAN. Thurso!

ALEX. Viking for 'dull'?

BRIAN. No.

ALEX. Bathgate by the sea.

48

Thurso. The SHAPER's workshop. A shrine of surf-boards.

ALEX *and* BRIAN *hesitate outside.* MIRREN *coaxes them in.*

MIRREN. What're you waiting out there for?

ALEX. Are you sure about this?

MIRREN. I phoned. He's expecting us.

They step into the workshop. Whispering.

BRIAN. What a place. Look at all those boards.

MIRREN. Don't touch anything.

ALEX. Sorry.

A noise in the corner.

MIRREN. Hello? Anybody in?

A beat.

SHAPER. Mistah Kurtz, he dead.

A beat.

MIRREN. Hello?

SHAPER. Hello.

The SHAPER emerges from the shadows.

SHAPER. That's better, eh? Mirren. Good to see you. Who're your friends?

MIRREN. These are the two guys I told you about.

SHAPER. Ah. The driver?

ALEX. Eh . . . yeah.

SHAPER. And the guide?

BRIAN. Yes.

SHAPER. You've come a long way.

BRIAN. From Motherwell. It's taken ages.

ALEX. The car's a wreck.

SHAPER. I saw it. Nice paint job, though.

MIRREN. Serge.

SHAPER. Of course.

BRIAN. It's been interesting.

ALEX. And slow.

SHAPER. 'All travelling becomes dull in exact proportion to its rapidity.' John Ruskin.

Pause.

SHAPER. What can I do for you?

ALEX. We need to sell a surf-board. Mirren thought you might be the best person to speak to.

SHAPER. About selling it?

ALEX. I think it's quite a good one. Quite expensive. But I don't know how much we might expect to get for it . . .

SHAPER. 'Money is our madness, our vast collective madness.'

BRIAN. D.H. Lawrence!

SHAPER. Absolutely correct, Mister . . .

The SHAPER *laughs.*

SHAPER. Mirren . . . ?

MIRREN. Sorry. This is Alex and this is Brian.

SHAPER. I'm Frank.

BRIAN. Do you think you'll be able to help us?

SHAPER. Have either of you ever surfed?

BRIAN. No.

ALEX. We're from Motherwell.

SHAPER. See, finding the right board isn't just about buying a lump of coloured resin. There's a relationship there. It's about compatability. Personality. Do you know what I mean?

ALEX. Not really.

SHAPER. What you've got to offer is a potential partner. A love affair. That's why you shouldn't put a price on it. You can't put a price on emotions can you, Alex?

ALEX. We need the money.

SHAPER. Ah. Separate problem entirely.

ALEX. So what do you suggest?

SHAPER. Well, you can't sell love. But there's no reason why you shouldn't expect an arrangement fee.

ALEX. A fee?

SHAPER. For bringing the happy couple together. Effecting the introduction. Oiling the cogs and wheels of the heart.

BRIAN. Matchmaking!

SHAPER. Precisely. It's not about making boards. Anybody can make a board. It's about making a good match. That's what people pay me for.

Pause.

ALEX. And you make a living from this?

MIRREN. People come from all over. He's world famous.

SHAPER. Only in Thurso.

MIRREN. Stop being so modest.

BRIAN. It's highly skilled then?

SHAPER. It's an art.

BRIAN. Can you learn it?

SHAPER. If you've got it, you can hone it. If you haven't got it . . .

BRIAN. How do you know if you've got it?

SHAPER. Difficult to say. You can usually tell by the colour of the light round your head.

A beat.

ALEX. So, will we be able to find a match for our board who might be suitably grateful?

SHAPER. We'll talk about it. But not before sunset.

BRIAN. Why not?

SHAPER. 'Cause I have to get to Safeways before it shuts.

49

A hotel in Thurso. BINKS *checks in.*

MO. Good evening, sir. Welcome to Thurso. What can I do for you?

BINKS. I need a room.

MO. Certainly. Single or double?

BINKS. Eh . . .

MO. Sir?

BINKS. Aye. Just a single. Of course.

MO. It's £45.00 a night including full breakfast . . .

BINKS. That's fine.

MO. If you'd just like to sign here. I'll get someone to take your luggage up for you.

BINKS. No luggage.

MO. None at all.

BINKS. No luggage!

MO. Okay then Mr . . . Yamaha. Your key. Breakfast is between seven and nine in the . . .

BINKS. All right Ron! I'll ask! . . . Fuck sake.

MO. Sir?

BINKS. Are there surfers in this place?

MO. Pardon?

BINKS. You know. Surfers.

MO. Yes.

BINKS. Where can I find them?

MO. Uhm . . . The beach.

BINKS. Apart fae the fucking beach. I mean where do they drink?

MO. Oh . . . Well there're a few places . . .

BINKS. Write them out for me and stick them under my door.

MO. Uh . . . Will there be anything else?

BINKS. I'll let you know.

MO. Second on the right at the top of the stairs, then.

BINKS. Ta.

50

The SHAPER *and the others having a drink in a bar.*

ALEX. D'you think she'll go for it?

SHAPER. Alex, it's a matter of alchemy. We'll find out tomorrow. She's nice, Mo. From Cornwall. Been up for about six months.

BRIAN. She came up here to surf. From Cornwall.

ALEX. Don't they have waves down there?

SHAPER. They're better up here.

ALEX. Colder too, I bet!

SHAPER. That's true. Straight down from the Arctic Circle. Huge. Monster waves. But absolutely fucking freezing. That's what always catches the sunshine boys out. Not quite Bondi.

BRIAN. They come from all over then?

SHAPER. Oh yeah. It's a key spot. Best waves in Europe on a good day.

ALEX. So how come no-one's heard of it?

SHAPER. You're here.

ALEX. That's a fluke.

SHAPER. It's 'cause it's not for tourists. You can't mess with the break around here. The waves are big but the water's icy. You can't stay out too long. And they come in over rock. If you get wiped-out you can really get wiped out.

ALEX. So why do they do it? If it's cold and dangerous? Why not go to California?

SHAPER. They're on a quest. That's why. They're looking for a wave.

ALEX. But there are waves all over.

SHAPER. They're looking for a particular wave. People come to me and I try and make the board that's right for them, their style of riding, even the particular break they want to surf in. I try and make the perfect match. But each combination'll be best suited for one particular wave. One ideal coming together of elements. One potentially perfect moment where everything in the universe is suddenly aligned. That's the wave they're looking for. That's the wave we're all looking for.

MIRREN. Does anybody find it?

SHAPER. It's not just a matter of finding it. You've got to recognise it when it comes and then you've got to have the courage to get up on it.

MIRREN. Is that what Mo's looking for?

SHAPER. Yep.

MIRREN. Will the board help her?

SHAPER. We'll know after she's tried it. I think they might hit it off.

Pause.

BRIAN. Is that why you came here? Looking for a wave.

SHAPER. Sort of.

BRIAN. Did you find it?

SHAPER. Aye. I found it. Or it found me.

BRIAN. What was it like?

SHAPER. Perfect. And brief. Her name was Elizabeth.

BRIAN. Oh.

SHAPER. It's just the same. It changes everything. What about you two? What're you looking for?

ALEX. Don't know.

SHAPER. A man who doesn't know what he's looking for is usually searching for himself.

BRIAN. Who said that?

SHAPER. Me.

Pause.

MIRREN. What time is Mo meeting us?

SHAPER. Seven.

ALEX. Shit.

SHAPER. You tired? Want to crash?

MIRREN. Yeah.

ALEX. Me too.

SHAPER. Brian?

BRIAN. I'm wide awake.

SHAPER. Well we can take a walk. You two can head back. The door's open. Mirren, you know where everything is.

MIRREN. Yeah. Okay.

ALEX. See you later.

BRIAN. See ya.

SHAPER. Sweet dreams.

    ALEX *and* MIRREN *leave.*

BRIAN. Are you trying to set them up?

SHAPER. Nothing so crude, Brian. It's part of the art. Trust me.

51

BINKS *in a different pub. He is drunk. He approaches the*
BARMAN.

BINKS. Oi. Barman. You a surfer?

BARMAN. Pardon?

BINKS. Surf! D'you surf, or what?

BARMAN. Sometimes.

BINKS. Anybody been in trying to sell a board?

BARMAN. No.

BINKS. Are you sure?

BARMAN. I think I would've noticed.

BINKS. They wouldn't have had it with them ya stupid prick!

BARMAN. If someone was selling a board, they'd be at the beach
    first thing in the morning. Not in here last thing at night.

BINKS. Is it late?

BARMAN. Yeah.

BINKS. Christ it was early when I started. Too many pubs.

BARMAN. Too many drinks.

BINKS. Are they surfers? Over there, with the hair?

BARMAN. Yeah. But I don't want you annoying them.

BINKS. Piss off.

52

ALEX *and* MIRREN *are walking home.*

MIRREN. Big day tomorrow then.

ALEX. Looks like it.

MIRREN. The end of the road.

ALEX. What'll you do?

MIRREN. Haven't decided yet. What about you?

ALEX. Haven't a clue.

Pause. ALEX *smiles.*

MIRREN. What?

ALEX. You're as fucked up as I am.

MIRREN *laughs.*

MIRREN. Never said I wasn't.

ALEX. I thought you were just a nippy bitch.

MIRREN. I thought you were just a sarky bastard.

ALEX *laughs.*

ALEX. I am.

MIRREN. Bastard.

ALEX. Bitch.

They both laugh.

53

BRIAN *and the* SHAPER *are walking by the sea.*

BRIAN. You know that stuff about the colour of the light in your head.

SHAPER. Yeah?

BRIAN. Well, how do you tell?

SHAPER. Good question. Complicated answer though. Let's go down by the water.

BRIAN. Yeah. All right.

SHAPER. ' . . . the sea delaying not, hurrying not whispered me through the night . . . '

BRIAN. Walt Whitman.

SHAPER. Brian, you're a man you don't meet every day.

BRIAN. Thanks.

54

Next day. The beach.

ALEX. The beach was long and wide and windswept.

BRIAN. Dunnet Bay.

ALEX. Five miles out of town.

BRIAN. The Lada slipped into the car park.

ALEX. Sighed a cloud of steam and oil-smoke . . .

BRIAN. . . . and then passed away.

A beat.

BRIAN. It was just after dawn. Cold . . .

ALEX. The waves were coming in like cavalry charges in a cheap western.

BRIAN. Frank and Mirren took the board down to Mo by the water.

ALEX. We stayed in the dunes and tried to keep out of the wind.

A beat.

BRIAN. And?

ALEX. And what?

BRIAN. What happened? Last night. You and Mirren.

ALEX. Nothing.

BRIAN. Nothing at all? Aye right. Go on. You can tell me.

ALEX. Nothing happened.

BRIAN *sniffs. He is unconvinced.*

ALEX. What did you do?

BRIAN. Went down by the castle and got stoned and talked a lot.

ALEX. About what?

BRIAN. Life.

ALEX. Fascinating.

BRIAN. He offered me a job.

ALEX. Eh?

BRIAN. Apprentice shaper. Sort of.

ALEX. Here?

BRIAN. Where else?

ALEX. Are you going to do it?

BRIAN. Yeah.

ALEX. So you really aren't going back?

BRIAN. Sorry. What will you do?

ALEX. I don't know.

    MIRREN *comes up the sand dune to join them.*

MIRREN. She's taking it out. Look. I think she likes it.

ALEX. Good.

MIRREN. It must be freezing out there though.

BRIAN. There's other folk out as well.

ALEX. Mad.

MIRREN. We're just as mad to be up this early watching them.

    The SHAPER *climbs up beside them too.*

SHAPER. She's giving it a go.

ALEX. She's well out.

BRIAN. She looks like a seal.

MIRREN. Why isn't she catching any of the waves?

SHAPER. She's waiting. You have to be patient.

    Pause.

ALEX. So there we stood, watching this tiny figure loitering in the swell. Waiting and waiting. The wind was making my eyes water and the sand was stinging my face. I was going to go back to the car and then I heard Frank make this sound like a very quiet moan. And I looked and Mo was moving now, paddling like mad on this lump of green water that was huge and getting bigger and bigger all the time . . .

BRIAN. Jesus.

MIRREN. It's massive!

SHAPER. And she's got it.

ALEX. She was hopping to her feet now on her board . . . our board . . . perched. It looked like she was standing on a plank stuck into the side of a railway embankment. And she was sliding down the face of this glass monster but it was moving so fast it looked as though she was standing still. And then she started to cut across it. Along its length. Swinging up to the lip and then zooming back down into the trough again and it seemed like the sea had stopped to watch her too . . .

SHAPER. Go on girl. That's the way . . .

MIRREN. It's amazing.

ALEX. It's . . . beautiful.

MIRREN. It is. Beautiful.

BRIAN. Chudovyi.

ALEX. And then it began to curl. To roll over on itself into a cylinder of foam. And she pointed herself into the tube and held it there under an overhang of wave.

BRIAN. Bloody hell.

ALEX. And she slipped into the tube so far that we could only see her outline through the wall of water. And everything was blurred. Her. The board. The wave. They merged.

SHAPER. Amazing!

ALEX. We watched all this. Spellbound. Nobody said a word. Until Mo finally came back up the beach.

MO *appears with the board.*

MO. Did you see it?

MIRREN. We saw.

BRIAN. It was spectacular.

SHAPER. Some wave.

MO. It was the one, Frank. That was it. It was just like you said. And the board was brilliant. Just perfect.

SHAPER. That's great.

ALEX. Does that mean you're going to take it?

MO. I can't. Not now.

ALEX. Why not?

MO. That was it, out there. You saw it. That was the one. It won't get any better with this board. Do you understand? I'm sorry.

BRIAN. It's all right.

MO. I am sorry. I'm sure you'll find someone else.

ALEX. Maybe.

MO. I better get dry. See ya later.

SHAPER. See ya.

She leaves. ALEX *is left holding the board.*

SHAPER. I suppose that match was a little too well made.

ALEX. It was perfect. She was right.

SHAPER. So what do you want to do with it now?

BINKS *has appeared behind them.*

BINKS. I'll take it off your hands.

They turn. BRIAN *yelps with shock.*

ALEX. What . . . What're you doing here?

BINKS. I'm on my holidays and thought I'd come for a paddle . . . !
What the fuck do you think I'm doing here dick-head?

MIRREN. You can't just . . .

BINKS. Oh yes I can. I can do whatever the fuck I want.

BINKS *pulls out his gun and cocks it.*

BRIAN. Fucking hell.

BINKS. Eh? . . . Aye . . . Right, bring that over here then back off.

ALEX *obeys.*

BINKS. You little pricks have put me to a lot of trouble.

ALEX. You've got it back now.

SHAPER. I don't mean to interrupt, but did you come on that
thing?

BINKS. What's it got to do with you?

SHAPER. Well, it'll be a bit difficult trying to carry a surf-board
three hundred miles on a motorbike.

BINKS. Who said I was here to take it back?

*He smashes the butt of his pistol against the board several
times until the fibre-glass splinters.*

SHAPER. You came all this way just to smash it up?

BINKS. Stay where you are.

BINKS *tugs at the splintered plastic and then laughs
triumphantly. He jingles a bag of coins at them.*

BINKS. What? . . . That's right . . . Ronnie says, you never even knew what you had. Did you? You stupid bastards. Think I'd come all this way for a fucking surf-board? I can't even fucking swim.

ALEX. So that's your pension fund.

BINKS. Got it in one shop-boy. Krugerands. South African gold . . .

SHAPER. I thought it felt a bit on the heavy side.

BRIAN. So you can go now?

BINKS. I haven't finished yet sunshine. There's some kneecap business to be done first.

ALEX. Oh shit.

SHAPER. Hold on a minute.

BINKS. Out of the way you, it's got nothing to do with you.

SHAPER. Course it has. I'm a witness.

BINKS. You'll be a dead witness if you don't get out of the way.

SHAPER. It's not a good idea.

BINKS. Eh? . . . Get back. Stand still I told you.

The SHAPER is moving slowly towards BINKS.

SHAPER. It's too risky.

BINKS. Stop . . . what you saying?

SHAPER. Listen to him.

BINKS. Shut up you . . . stand still . . . Who you talking about?

SHAPER. Listen to him. He's right.

BINKS. Fucking shut up. Shut up or I'll blow your head off . . . What?

SHAPER. Ronnie says it's too risky.

A pause. BINKS is taken aback.

BINKS. You can hear him?

SHAPER. Every word.

BINKS. You can hear Ronnie?

SHAPER. He's telling you it's too dangerous. Too many witnesses. No chance of getting away.

BINKS. You can!

SHAPER. You should listen to him.

BINKS. But . . . how can . . .

SHAPER. 'Cause I'm like you. We're special you and me. Chosen. And Ronnie's smart. He knows what he's talking about.

BINKS. He is. He's fucking smart.

SHAPER. It was his idea to hide the gold.

BINKS. Sharp as a knife.

SHAPER. And now he thinks you should put down the gun.

Listen to him. Take the money and go.

But put down the gun.

BINKS. I . . . I . . . What? . . . I don't know . . . I can't . . .

SHAPER. That's it. No rush. It's easy.

BINKS. Stay there . . . I . . . I can't hear you . . . Ron . . . ?

SHAPER. He says don't be stupid.

BINKS. Ron . . . ?

SHAPER. He says it's time to go.

BINKS. Ronnie! Where are you?

BINKS is immensely distressed and confused. He starts to cry quietly.

MIRREN. He's mad.

BINKS hears her whisper and is suddenly raging again.

BINKS. No! You're the mad ones. You're off your fucking heads up here. All of you. Every last sheep-shagging bastard. D'you hear me? Every. Last. One.

The gun goes off with a huge noise. MIRREN screams. BINKS legs it. A beat.

ALEX. Frank? Are you all right?

SHAPER. I'm in a better state than that poor guy.

A motorbike revs and roars off.

ALEX. He was going to kill you.

SHAPER. He wouldn't hurt me. I knew his brother.

MIRREN. You mean you really did hear the voices?

ALEX. I don't believe it.

SHAPER. Mr Binks believed it.

ALEX. But who did he shoot at then?

BRIAN. Look at the car.

The car is burning.

MIRREN. Oh no.

ALEX. Brian. He's killed it.

BRIAN. It was dead already

ALEX. Maybe George can claim on his insurance. Say it was joyriders.

BRIAN. At least he'll never see the paint-job.

The petrol tank explodes with a boom.

SHAPER. Looks like we're walking back to town, then.

BRIAN. Looks like it . . . You coming.

ALEX. In a minute.

BRIAN *and* ALEX *share a look for a moment.* BRIAN *turns and he and the* SHAPER *begin to head off.* ALEX *kicks at the bits of the broken surf-board.*

ALEX. It's a shame. All that way for this.

MIRREN. At least it found its one wave.

ALEX. I suppose so.

MIRREN. What now?

ALEX. Don't know. Maybe I'll just keep going north.

MIRREN. Out there?

ALEX. Orkney. Shetland. Scandinavia.

MIRREN. I'm going that way.

ALEX. Yeah? Maybe we could . . .

MIRREN. Maybe.

ALEX. I'd like that. I'd like to be able to say 'beautiful' in Swedish.

Pause.

MIRREN. What you thinking?

ALEX. I'm not. I'm not thinking at all. I'm just letting it happen.

Wind. Waves. Burning car.

Fade to black.

End.

A Nick Hern Book

Passing Places first published in Great Britain as
an original paperback in 1998 by Nick Hern Books Limited,
14 Larden Road, London W3 7ST, in association with
the Traverse Theatre, Edinburgh

Passing Places copyright © 1998 Stephen Greenhorn

Cover image by Euan Myles

Typeset by Country Setting, Woodchurch, Kent TN26 3TB
Printed in England by Cox & Wyman Ltd, Reading, Berks

ISBN 185459 349 8

A CIP catalogue record for this book is available from
the British Library